LATIN FOR
LOCAL HISTORY

An Introduction

EILEEN A. GOODER

LONGMANS

LONGMANS, GREEN AND CO LTD
48 Grosvenor Street, London W1

*Associated companies, branches and representatives
throughout the world*

© *Eileen A. Gooder 1961*
First Published 1961
Third Impression 1967

*Printed in Great Britain by
Butler and Tanner Ltd, Frome and London*

To my Mother and Father

ACKNOWLEDGEMENTS

Thanks are due first to Mr. E. Saunders, for whom, amongst other students, this course was devised, and who by his continuing interest and application encouraged me also to continue; to Mr. E. R. C. Brinkworth, M.A., B.Litt., for a valuable contribution of ecclesiastical vocabulary; to Mr. Terrick Fitz-Hugh of *The Amateur Historian* for his encouragement at a difficult period; and to my husband, without whose help the last lap would never have been completed.

FOREWORD

This course is aimed at enabling students whose knowledge of Latin is weak or non-existent to understand medieval Latin as it occurs in local records: practice is given in *reading only* as it is obviously unnecessary for the local historian to be trained to *write* Latin.

It is based wholly upon records material, and should enable the student to understand deeds, charters, manor and borough court rolls, and accounts in particular. Items from bishops' registers, chapter act books, etc., are also included. Practice material in general has been selected to illustrate grammatical points and to give as wide and varied a grasp of the language as possible, rather than in an attempt to cover all forms of all records, as this is manifestly impossible in the compass of one volume.

The practice material is culled directly from documents and should be regarded as extending the scope of the preliminary explanations, as it contains many additional points which can best be made clear in the context of sentences; it culminates in the full examples of documents given in the formulary.

The Word List is an integral part of the book, containing much additional information, conveyed more economically in this way than in additional chapters of text. For further comments on the Word List see its Preface.

NOTE. This text-book is intended to be used in conjunction with *The Shorter Latin Primer* (by B. H. Kennedy, rev. by J. W. Bartram. Longmans, 1931).

CONTENTS

ABBREVIATIONS

abl.	ABLATIVE	infin.	INFINITIVE
absol.	ABSOLUTE	leg.	LEGAL
acc.	ACCUSATIVE	lit.	LITERALLY
adj.	ADJECTIVE	m.	MASCULINE
adv.	ADVERB	n.	NEUTER
conj.	CONJUNCTION	nom.	NOMINATIVE
conjug.	CONJUGATION	part.	PARTICIPLE
dat.	DATIVE	pl.	PLURAL
decl.	DECLENSION	prep.	PREPOSITION
depon.	DEPONENT	pres.	PRESENT
eccles.	ECCLESIASTICAL	pron.	PRONOUN
f.	FEMININE	sg.	SINGULAR
gen.	GENITIVE	subj.	SUBJUNCTIVE

The numbers after verbs indicate their conjugation.

I

Introduction; *Do, Terra*

---

1. Observe the English verb 'to give':

SINGULAR	PLURAL
1. I give	1. we give
2. you give	2. you give
3. he, she, it, gives	3. they give

and notice the change in the verb in the third person singular.

Latin verbs change for all persons:

SINGULAR		PLURAL	
do	I give	*damus*	we give
das	you give	*datis*	you give
dat	he, she, it, gives	*dant*	they give

so that it is not necessary to put in the pronouns (I, you, he, etc.) and they are often omitted.

NOTE. Latin makes the distinction between 'you' (singular, i.e., thou) and 'you' (plural, i.e., more than one person). But in local records (excepting certain ecclesiastical forms), 'you' occurs much less frequently than the other persons, and the student may safely pay greater attention to the latter throughout the course.

2. English nouns change only in three ways:

e.g., land
     lands (plural)
     land's (meaning 'of the land', as in Land's End)
     lands' ('of the lands')

Latin nouns change to convey a number of meanings:

SINGULAR		PLURAL
terra	land (as subject of a sentence: 'the land is a hard task-master')	*terre*
terram	land (as object of a verb: 'he tills the land')	*terras*

SINGULAR		PLURAL
terre	of the land	
terre	to the land	*terrarum*
terra	by, with, from, the land	*terris*
		terris

It will be noticed that: (*a*) some of the forms above appear to be the same but bear different meanings. In practice, the cast of the sentence in which the word appears makes the particular meaning clear. (*b*) Latin lacks the definite and indefinite articles, i.e. 'the', and 'a' or 'an'. One must supply these in translation, according to the context.

3. A Latin sentence often has its verb at the end. Hence a short sentence might run:

Terram filie dat—He (or she) gives land to the daughter (*filia*—a daughter)

PRACTICE

ego—I (the persons are sometimes expressed)
virgata—a virgate (about 30 acres of land)

1. *Terras filie das.* You (i.e., thou) give lands to the daughter
2. *Terram filie damus.* We give land to the daughter.
3. *Filia terram dat.* The daughter gives land.
4. *Ego filie terram do.* I give land to the daughter.
5. *Virgatam terre filie datis.* You (plural) give a virgate of land to the daughter.

2

Cases; *Dominus, Filius, Filia*

1. Case endings

The different inflexions of Latin nouns are called cases, and it is convenient to have names for them for reference. They are:

> Nominative—subject of sentence.
> Accusative—object of verb.
> Genitive—possessive—of a thing.
> Dative—to a thing, for a thing.
> Ablative—by, with, from, a thing.

NOTE. The second meaning of the dative is less common in medieval Latin; 'for a thing' is generally expressed by *pro* with the ablative case.

2. Second group of nouns

The nouns we have had so far end in -*a*. A second group ends in -*us*:

> e.g., *dominus*—a lord

	SINGULAR	PLURAL
Nom.	*dominus*	*domini*
Acc.	*dominum*	*dominos*
Gen.	*domini*	*dominorum*
Dat.	*domino*	*dominis*
Abl.	*domino*	*dominis*

> *filius*—a son

	SINGULAR	PLURAL
N.	*filius*	*filii*
A.	*filium*	*filios*
G.	*filii*	*filiorum*
D.	*filio*	*filiis*
A.	*filio*	*filiis*

3. Declensions

There are five main different types of nouns, and the term used to distinguish them is 'declension'. Nouns ending in -*a*, like *filia*, are first declension; nouns like *dominus* and *filius* are second declension.

4. Plural of *filia*

Because of the possibility of confusion in the dative and ablative plural of *filius* and *filia*, the latter has an irregular dative and ablative plural, borrowed from the third declension:

PLURAL

N.	*filie*	D.	*filiabus*
A.	*filias*	A.	*filiabus*
G.	*filiarum*		

PRACTICE

1. *Dominus terras filiis dat.*
2. *Domini tres virgatas terre filiabus dant.*
3. *Filia Elizabetha tres acras terre domino dat (tres,* three; *acra,* acre).
4. *Filii decem acras terre dominis dant (decem,* ten).
5. *Dominus decem acras terrarum suarum* (his) *filio dat.*

TRANSLATION*

1. The lord gives lands to the sons.
2. The lords give three virgates of land to the daughters.
3. The daughter Elizabeth gives three acres of land to the lord.
4. The sons give ten acres of land to the lords.
5. The lord gives ten acres of his (*suarum*) lands to the son.

* In each chapter the practice sentences are followed by their translation.

4

3

Second-declension neuters *Pratum*, *Messuagium*; gender

---

1. The second declension has another type of noun:

e.g., *pratum*—a meadow, and *messuagium*—a messuage

	SINGULAR		PLURAL	
N.	*pratum*	*messuagium*	*prata*	*messuagia*
A.	*pratum*	*messuagium*	*prata*	*messuagia*
G.	*prati*	*messuagii*	*pratorum*	*messuagiorum*
D.	*prato*	*messuagio*	*pratis*	*messuagiis*
A.	*prato*	*messuagio*	*pratis*	*messuagiis*

2. So far we have had nouns ending in -*a*, -*us*, -*um*, and we come to the question of gender of nouns.

(*a*) Obviously *filia*, a daughter, is feminine.

(*b*) Obviously *filius*, a son, is masculine; BUT

(*c*) By a grammatical convention, all Latin nouns are either masculine, feminine, or neuter in gender, even in the case of words not referring to sex:

e.g., *carta*—paper, a deed, a charter—feminine
annus—a year—masculine

(*d*) Nouns of first declension, ending in -*a*, are feminine (e.g., *via*—a road, feminine), with the exception of one or two which by their nature are masculine, as: *parsona*—a parson, masculine.

(*e*) Nouns ending in -*us* of second declension are masculine, as: *dominus*—a lord, masculine, and also *locus*—a place.

(*f*) Nouns ending in -*um* of second declension are neuter in gender: *regnum*—a reign, neuter.

PRACTICE

1. *Dominus messuagium et pratum filio dat.*
2. *Parsona cartam domino dat.*
3. *Novem acras prati filie damus (novem, nine).*
4. *Ego unum (one) messuagium filie Elizabethe do.*
5. *Dominus et parsona terras et prata dant.*

5

1. The lord gives a messuage and meadow to the son.
2. The parson gives the charter to the lord.
3. We give nine acres of meadow to the daughter.
4. I give one messuage to the daughter Elizabeth.
5. The lord and the parson give lands and meadows.

4

Adjectives: declension and agreement; *Predictus*; *Dedi*

1. Adjectives must 'agree' with their nouns in number (i.e., singular or plural), gender, and case as:

> the aforesaid lord—*predictus dominus*
> of the aforesaid lord—*predicti domini*
> of the aforesaid lords—*predictorum dominorum*

2. There are two main groups of adjectives, and those of the first group have three forms (like the regular nouns of first and second declensions) to 'agree' with masculine, feminine, and neuter nouns:

> e.g., *predictus*—aforesaid

| | SINGULAR | | | | PLURAL | | |
	Masc.	Fem.	Neut.		Masc.	Fem.	Neut.
N.	*predictus*	*-a*	*-um*		*-i*	*-e*	*-a*
A.	*predictum*	*-am*	*-um*		*-os*	*-as*	*-a*
G.	*predicti*	*-e*	*-i*		*-orum*	*-arum*	*-orum*
D.	*predicto*	*-e*	*-o*		*-is*	*-is*	*-is*
A.	*predicto*	*-a*	*-o*		*-is*	*-is*	*-is*

3. So: the aforesaid son—*predictus filius*
> the aforesaid daughter—*predicta filia*
> the aforesaid meadow—*predictum pratum*
> BUT the aforesaid parson—*predictus parsona*
> to the aforesaid sons—*predictis filiis*
> BUT to the aforesaid daughters—*predictis filiabus*

i.e., the adjective often has the same ending as the noun, but not necessarily. The number, case and gender of the noun are the guides.

4. The past tense of *dare*, 'to give', is as follows:

	SINGULAR		PLURAL	
dedi	I gave	*dedimus*	we gave	
	(or have given)		(or have given)	
dedisti	you gave	*dedistis*	you gave	
	(or have given)		(or have given)	

SINGULAR	PLURAL

dedit he, she, it gave   *dederunt* they gave

       (or has given)   (or have given)

PRACTICE

1. *Ursula predicta* (the adjective often comes after its noun) *decem acras terrarum dedit filiis predictis Roberto et Radulpho.*

2. *Dominus Rogerus predictum messuagium ecclesie Sancte Marie dedit* (*sanctus, sancta, sanctum,* adjective—holy, saint; *ecclesia,* feminine noun—church).

3. *Domini predicti prata predicta dederunt filiabus predictis Elizabethe et Juliane.*

4. *Nos* (we) *predicti* (masc., plur., nom.) *Willelmus et Robertus predictas decem acras terre in Eccleshall situatas parsone predicto Philippo dedimus* (*situatus, -a, -um,* adjective—situated).

5. *Dominus Gilebertus tres virgatas terre predictas filio Ricardo dat.*

1. The aforesaid Ursula gave (or has given) ten acres of lands to the aforesaid sons Robert and Ralph. (NOTE. Roberto and Radulpho in dative: the names stand beside the noun *filiis* to make its meaning clear, and 'agree' in a similar way to adjectives; in this case, however, 'sons' is plural, Roberto and Radulpho each singular, because there is only one Robert and one Ralph.)

2. The lord Roger gave the aforesaid messuage to the church of Saint Mary.

3. The aforesaid lords gave the aforesaid meadows to (the) aforesaid daughters, Elizabeth and Juliana.

4. We, the aforesaid William and Robert gave the aforesaid ten acres of land situated in Eccleshall to the aforesaid parson Philip.

5. The lord Gilbert gives the aforesaid three virgates of land to the son Richard.

8

5

Hic; past perfect; *Confirmo*

1. The following declension of the pronoun *hic*, meaning 'this', should be compared with the declension as set out in Kennedy's *Shorter Latin Primer*, p. 31. The *Primer* will be used from now on as a book of reference. It will be seen that the forms with *ae* in Kennedy are given here with *e* only; this is one of the differences between classical and medieval practice, which holds good for all types of word.

NOTE. The revival of classical Latin in Renaissance times gives rise to the reappearance of the *ae* forms.

	SINGULAR			PLURAL		
	M.	**F.**	**N.**	**M.**	**F.**	**N.**
N.	hic	hec	hoc	hi	he	hec
A.	hunc	hanc	hoc	hos	has	hec
G.	huius	huius	huius	horum	harum	horum
D.	huic	huic	huic	his*	his*	his*
A.	hoc	hac	hoc	his*	his*	his*

Certain similarities with first and second declension will be seen, especially in the plural masculine and feminine nominative and accusative, and all genders in genitive, dative, and ablative. Notice that nominative and accusative, both singular and plural, of the neuter forms, are the same: this characteristic holds good for all neuter words.

2. Compare the following forms of the verb *confirmare*, 'to confirm', with Kennedy, p. 42, where the verb *amare*, 'to love', is given as a model.

PRESENT	PAST (PERFECT)
confirmo (I confirm)	*confirmavi* (I confirmed or have confirmed)
confirmas	*confirmavisti*
confirmat	*confirmavit*
confirmamus	*confirmavimus*

* Often given as *hiis* in medieval Latin.

9

PRESENT	PAST (PERFECT)
confirmatis	*confirmavistis*
confirmant	*confirmaverunt*

The present tense and the past (called the perfect) should be studied. It will be seen that *amo, do* (I give), and *confirmo* all follow the same pattern in the present, and that *amo* and *confirmo* are similar in their past tenses, while *do* has the same endings in the past, but a different root. The endings are the same for all verbs in the past tense, although the basic root differs:

SINGULAR	PLURAL
-i (I)	*-imus* (we)
-isti (you)	*-istis* (you)
-it (he, she, it)	*-erunt* (they)

Amo and *confirmo* are typical examples of regular verbs of the first conjugation,* and their root in the past tense ends in *-av*, to which the endings as above are added. *Do* is an irregular verb, and its root for the past tense is *ded*, to which the endings are added.

PRACTICE

1. *Has predictas sex virgatas terre predictus Robertus dedit et hac carta confirmavit ecclesie Sancti Philippi* (*sex*—six; *septem*—seven; *octo*—eight: these do not decline).

2. *Alicia filia predicti domini Rogeri terram predictam dat et hac carta confirmat ecclesie Sancti Leonardi.*

3. *Nos Ricardus et Radulfus predictas septem acras predictum messuagium et unum pratum situatum in Whitley dedimus et hac carta confirmavimus ecclesie Sancte Marie* (*unus*—one: does decline).

4. *Domini Gilebertus et Willelmus hec predicta prata hoc predictum messuagium et has predictas octo acras terre in Coventre situatas dederunt et hac carta confirmaverunt predicto parsone Henrico.*

1. The aforesaid Robert has given and by this charter confirmed these aforesaid six virgates of land to the church of St. Philip.

2. Alice, daughter of the aforesaid lord Roger, gives and by this charter confirms the aforesaid land to the church of St. Leonard.

3. We, Richard and Ralph, have given and by this charter con-

* There are four main types of verbs; they are grouped as first, second, third and fourth conjugations.

firmed, the aforesaid seven acres, the aforesaid messuage, and one meadow situated in Whitley, to the church of St. Mary.

4. The lords Gilbert and William have given and by this charter confirmed these aforesaid meadows, this aforesaid messuage, and these aforesaid eight acres of land situated in Coventry, to the aforesaid parson, Henry.

6

Second declension, cont., *Magister*; *Noster*; prepositions (*In*, etc.)

---

1. Second declension, continued. A small group of words end in *-es* (instead of *-us*, like *dominus*), e.g., *magister*, 'master', but in the cases other than nominative, they drop the *e*. For full declension or *magister*, see Kennedy, p. 8. (NOTE. Readers of this book can safely disregard all vocative cases.) *Faber*, 'a smith', declines like *magister*.

2. There is a small group of adjectives similar to these nouns, which decline like *niger* (Kennedy, p. 21). REMINDER: *ae* in classical Latin becomes *e* in medieval.

   > *noster, nostra, nostrum*—our
   > *vester, vestra, vestrum*—your (more than one person)
   > *eger, egra, egrum*—ill, sick

3. A few words decline as above without dropping the *e*: e.g., *armiger*, 'esquire' (like *puer*, Kennedy, p. 8); *liber, libera, liberum*, adjective, 'free' (like *tener*, Kennedy, p. 21).

4. A dictionary or word list gives guidance as to the way words behave:

   (*a*) Nouns are given in the nominative case, followed by the genitive, generally abbreviated, then the gender, then the meaning (e.g., *magister, -tri*, m., 'master'). The genitive form is the key to the formation of the other cases, i.e., in the word *magister* the *e* is dropped.

   (*b*) Adjectives are given in masculine, feminine, and neuter forms, generally abbreviated, e.g., *predictus, -a, -um*, adj., 'aforesaid', BUT *noster, -tra, -trum*, adj., 'our'; here the feminine and neuter forms indicate that the *e* is dropped in all cases and genders except nominative masculine singular.

5. The following prepositions with nouns in the ablative case give special meanings: *in*—in, into, on; *cum*—with; *de*—from, concerning; *pro*—on behalf of, in accordance with; *ex*—from, out of;

coram—in the presence of; *ab* (generally given as *a* before a consonant)—by, from; *sine*—without.

PRACTICE

1. *Nos Christoferus et Constancia uxor mea damus et hac nostra carta confirmamus Willelmo et Roberto filiis nostris unum messuagium cum terris pratis pasturis et pertinentiis universis modo in tenura Reginaldi.*

2. *Nos Willelmus et Ricardus Judd dedimus et hac nostra carta confirmavimus Rogero fabro unam parcellam terre in Coventre situatam.*

3. *Nos Johannes et Margareta prefatis filiis nostris Edwardo et Philippo damus et hac nostra carta confirmamus supranominatas clausuras pasturas et quinque parcellas prati.*

4. *Ego Walterus supradicto Henrico quattuor parcellas terre dedi et hoc scripto confirmavi.*

nos—we. *uxor mea*—my wife. *pastura*—pasture. *pertinentia*—an appurtenance. *modo*—now. *universus, -a, -um*, adj.—all. *tenura*—tenure. *parcella*—a parcel. *prefatus, -a, -um*, adj.—aforesaid. *supranominatus, -a, -um*, adj.—above-named. *clausura*—a close. *supradictus, -a, -um*, adj.—above-named, aforesaid. *scriptum*—a writing, a deed. *quattuor* (does not decline)—four. *quinque* (does not decline)—five.

1. We, Christopher and Constance my wife, give and by this our charter confirm to William and Robert our sons, one messuage with lands, meadows, pastures, and all appurtenances, now in the tenure of Reginald.

2. We, William and Richard Judd, have given and by this our charter confirmed to Roger the smith, one parcel of land situated in Coventry.

3. We, John and Margaret, give and by this our charter confirm to our aforesaid sons Edward and Philip, the above-named closes, pastures, and five parcels of meadow.

4. I, Walter, have given and by this writing confirmed to the above-named Henry, four parcels of land.

7

Pronouns; *Ullus, Alter, Is,* etc.

A group of pronouns follows the general lines of the first and second declensions to give the masculine, feminine, and neuter forms, BUT

the dative singular ends in -*i*
the genitive singular ends in -*ius*

They can be subdivided as follows:

(*a*) Ending in -*us,* -*a,* -*um*:
ullus, -*a,* -*um*—any; *solus,* -*a,* -*um*—only, sole; *totus,* -*a,* -*um*—all, the whole; *nullus,* -*a,* -*um*—none, no; *unus,* -*a,* -*um*—one

(*b*) Ending in -*er*:
alter, altera, alterum—the other (of two things)
uter, utra, utrum—which (of two things)
neuter, neutra, neutrum—neither (of two things)

(*c*) Ending variously:
alius, alia, aliud—other, another
is, ea, id—he, she, it; this or that (man, woman, thing)
ille, illa, illud—he, she, it; that
iste, ista, istud—this (man, woman, thing)
ipse, ipsa, ipsum—he himself, she herself, itself
idem, eadem, idem—the same (man, woman, thing)
this is really *is, ea, id,* with the special ending *dem* added, and contracted to ease pronunciation.

The precise meanings and use of these pronouns will become clear with practice. Their full declensions will be found in Kennedy, pp. 31, 32, 34, but NOTE that the genitive singular of *alius*, given there as *alius*, should be disregarded: *alterius,* borrowed from *alter*, is used, to avoid confusion with the nominative masculine singular.

PRACTICE

1. *Ego Gilebertus Bolton armiger dedi et hac carta mea confirmavi Ricardo filio meo unum messuagium cum pertinentiis universis in Howton nominatum Kirkeplace modo in tenura Willelmi Kirke.*

14

2. *Elena uxor Gileberti Bolton armigeri totas illas terras prenominatas in illa parochia filie Alicie dedit et hac carta confirmavit.*

3. *Ego Johannes Whitaker de parochia de Whitfield, faber, pro anima filii mei Rogeri modo defuncti, dedi unam clausuram cum prato ecclesie Sancti Jacobi.*

4. *Hec concordia facta est* (was made) *coram Justiciariis Roberto Bolton et Radulfo Poole.*

5. *Post decessum prefati Ricardi illud messuagium cum universis pertinentiis ad nos revertetur* (shall revert to us) *sine ulla calumpnia vel retenemento.*

NOTE. From now on new words should be looked up in the word list at the end of this book.

1. I, Gilbert Bolton, esquire, have given and by this my charter confirmed to Richard my son one messuage with all appurtenances in Howton, named Kirkeplace [i.e., the name of the messuage] now in the tenure of William Kirke.

2. Ellen, wife of Gilbert Bolton, esquire, has given and by this charter confirmed all those lands aforenamed in that parish to the daughter Alice.

3. I, John Whitaker of* the parish of Whitfield, smith, for the sake of the soul of my son Roger, now dead, gave one close with meadow to the church of St. James.

4. This agreement was made before the Justices Robert Bolton and Ralph Poole.

5. After the death of the aforesaid Richard, that messuage with all appurtenances shall revert to us without any claim or reservation.

* *de*, literally meaning *from*, is translated *of* in this kind of phrase.

8

Meus, Suus, Eius

---

1. *Meus, mea, meum*, adj.—my
   suus, sua, suum, adj.—his, her, its, their
   decline like *predictus, -a, -um*, or like *bonus, -a, -um* (Kennedy, p. 20;
   note *ae* becomes *e* in medieval Latin).

2. *Suus* refers

   (*a*) to the subject of the sentence:

   Gilebertus suam terram filio suo dat—G. gives his land to his son.
   Alicia suam terram filio suo dat—A. gives her land to her son.
   G. et A. suam terram filio suo dant—G. and A. give their land to
   their son.
   Messuagium cum suis pertinenciis—a messuage with its appurte-
   nances.
   Ille terre cum suis pertinenciis—those lands with their appurte-
   nances.

   (*b*) to the leading noun of the phrase in which it occurs:

   Dominus illas terras cum suis pertinenciis filio suo dedit.

   The lord gave those lands with their appurtenances to his son.

   In practice it is generally obvious how to translate *suus*.

3. BUT NOTE, the genitive of *is, ea, id*, is also used to mean 'his', 'her',
   'its', 'their':
   Alicia et maritus eius—Alice and the husband of her, i.e., Alice and
   her husband.
   Gilebertus et uxor eius—Gilbert and the wife of him, i.e., G. and his
   wife.
   A. et G. et filius eorum—A. and G. and the son of them, i.e., their son.

4. NOTE preposition *ad* with accusative, meaning 'towards', 'to':
   ad terminum vite sue—to, up to, the end of his life (generally translated 'for the term of his life').
   ad totam vitam predicte Alicie—for the whole life of the aforesaid Alice.

PRACTICE

1. *Ego Johannes de Halton armiger dedi et hac mea carta confirmavi Willelmo filio meo ad terminum vite sue universas terras modo in tenura Isolde Bell vidue.*

2. *Ego ipse Henricus Travers dedi et carta mea confirmavi prefato Ricardo ad totam vitam suam totas illas terras cum pertinenciis eorum situatas in villa de Brough.*

3. *Ego prenominata Elizabetha, uxor Roberti Whittaker, do et hoc scripto meo confirmo Marie filie mee ad terminum vite sue unum cotagium cum pertinenciis suis situatum in illa villa prefata.*

4. *Ego Randulfus, filius Talboti, et Matilda uxor mea dedimus et hac nostra carta confirmavimus Herberto clerico de Wolvey pro homagio et servicio suo croftum nostrum in Brandon cum prato et aliis pertinenciis.*

5. *Ricardus de Selden et uxor eius dederunt et hoc scripto confirmaverunt Thome* de Bedeley totam terram suam cum pertinenciis in Selden, videlicet unam peciam terre nominatam Jocemedwe cum universis pertinenciis suis.*

1. I, John de Halton, esquire, have given and by this my charter confirmed to William my son for the term of his life all the lands now in the tenure of Isolda Bell, widow.

2. I myself, Henry Travers, have given and by my charter confirmed to the aforesaid Richard for his whole life all those lands with their appurtenances situated in the vill of Brough.

3. I, the aforenamed Elizabeth, wife of Robert Whittaker, give and by this my deed confirm to Mary my daughter for the term of her life one cottage with its appurtenances, situated in that vill aforesaid.

4. I, Randolf, son of Talbot, and Matilda my wife, have given and by this our charter confirmed to Herbert, clerk of Wolvey, for his homage and service our croft in Brandon with the meadow and other appurtenances.

5. Richard de Selden and his wife have given and by this deed confirmed to Thomas de Bedeley all their land with appurtenances in Selden, namely one piece of land named Jocemedwe with all its appurtenances.

* See Word List for declension of Thomas, first declension but masculine.

9

Qui, Que, Quod; second conjugation; *Habeo*

---

1. *Qui, que, quod*—who, which.

For declension, see Kennedy, p. 32. Note similarities with pronouns in Chapter 8, i.e., genitive in *-ius*, dative in *-i*, and the plural like regular first- and second-declension words, except for dative and ablative: *quibus* (disregard *quis*, given in Kennedy as alternative), which is a third-declension form, already seen in *filiabus* and *animabus*.*

Illustrations of its use

who— subject ∴ nom.	M.	J. is the son who (*filius qui*) inherits the land.
	F.	A. is the daughter who (*filia que*) inherits the land.
	N.	This is the meadow which (*pratum quod*) is his.

whom— object ∴ acc.	J. is the son whom (*filius quem*) his father assaulted.
	A. is the daughter whom (*filia quam*) he married.
	This is the meadow which (*pratum quod*) I granted.

whose— of whom ∴ gen.	J. is the son whose (i.e., of whom: *filius cuius*) wife is Alice.
	A. is the daughter whose (*filia cuius*) husband is John.
	This is the meadow whose (of which: *pratum cuius*) boundaries adjoin his.

to whom— ∴ dat.	J. is the son to whom (*filius cui*) I grant this.
	A. is the daughter to whom (*filia cui*) I grant this.
	This is the messuage to which (*messuagium cui*) the meadow belongs.

ablative after *a* and *in*	J. is the son from whom (*filius a quo*) I received the rent.
	A. is the daughter from whom (*filia a qua*) I received the rent.
	This is the meadow in which (*pratum in quo*) the beasts were found.

* Students are advised to master the pronouns by constant reference to Kennedy during practice rather than to attempt to learn them by rote.

It takes the number and gender of the word to which it refers, BUT its case is governed by the way it stands in its own phrase.

2. *The second group (conjugation) of verbs*

Where the first group has *a* as the characteristic vowel of the present tense (*das, dat, damus, datis, dant*) the second group has *e*, with the same endings; see Kennedy, p. 44, where *moneo* is given as the model.

NOTE past tense: the root alters to *monu-*, but the same endings as met in *confirmavi* and *dedi* are then added.

Examples: *habeo*—I have   *habui*—I had
           teneo—I hold   *tenui*—I held
           iaceo—I lie   *iacui*—I lay

PRACTICE

1. *Johannes Daye dedit Willelmo Warde et Alicie uxori eius et Willelmo filio eorum unum messuagium et tres acras terre cum pertinenciis suis in Brayton; quarum una acra iacet in Southfield iuxta terram Walteri Lynes et una acra iacet in Lytelfield et una acra iacet in Langefurlonge iuxta terram Roberti Bladon.*

2. *Rogerus Balle dedit Thome Wylson et Margarete uxori eius et Isabelle filie predicti Thome unum messuagium unam acram et dimidiam terre arrabilis* (arable) *et unam rodam prati cum pertinenciis, quarum dimidia acra iacet inter terram Alberti Woodyarde et terram Walteri filii eius, et una dimidia iacet in le Northfelde inter terram domini de Hampton et terram Roberti Haye, et dimidia acra iacet in campo de Hampton et predicta roda prati iacet in prato communi* (common) *de Merston.*

3. *Ego Simo de Whitney, faber, dedi et hac mea carta confirmavi Roberto filio Arnaldi pro homagio et servicio suo et pro iiii marcis argenti totam terram meam quam habui in Blakefurlong et pratum quod iacet in parochia de Witney.*

4. *Ego Mauricius dedi Jordano de Barston unam virgatam terre videlicet illam quam Edmundus de Coten nuper tenuit.*

1. J. D. gave to W. W. and to Alice his wife and William their son one messuage and three acres of land with their appurtenances in Brayton; of which one acre lies in Southfield next the land of Walter Lynes and one acre lies in Lytelfield and one acre lies in Langefurlonge next the land of Robert Bladon.

2. R. B. gave to Thomas Wylson and Margaret his wife and Isabella,

daughter of the aforesaid Thomas, one messuage, one acre and a half of arable land and one rood of meadow with appurtenances, of which a half acre lies between the land of A. W. and the land of Walter his son, and one half lies in the Northfelde between the land of the lord of Hampton and the land of Robert Haye, and a half acre lies in the field of Hampton, and the aforesaid rood of meadow lies in the common meadow of Merston.

3. I, Simon de Whitney, smith, have given and by this my charter confirmed to Robert son of Arnold, for his homage and service and for four marks of silver all my land which I had in Blakefurlong and the meadow which lies in the parish of Witney.

4. I, M., gave to J. de B. one virgate of land, namely that which E. de C. lately held.

IO

Third-declension nouns and adjectives

(a) Nouns: all three genders occur.

Nominative singular—many different forms. The other cases incorporate the true root plus the set of endings as below:

	SINGULAR		PLURAL	
	M. F.	N.	M. F.	N.
N.	Various	Various	*-es*	*-a*
A.	*-em*	Same as nom.	*-es*	*-a*
G.	*-is*	*-is*	*-um*	*-um*
D.	*-i*	*-i*	*-ibus*	*-ibus*
A.	*-e*	*-e*	*-ibus*	*-ibus*

e.g., *pater, -tris*, m., father: root *patr-*, declension: see Kennedy,
p. 14.
nomen, -inis, n., name: root *nomin-*, declension: see Kennedy,
p. 14.
miles, -itis, m., a knight: root *milit-*, declension: see Kennedy,
p. 12.

A few nouns have *-ium* in genitive plural; these are specially noted in the Word List. The very small number of exceptional neuter nouns are also specially noted (e.g., *altare*—an altar; see Word List); these behave like neuter adjectives.

(b) Adjectives: behave like nouns EXCEPT for ablative singular in *-i*, genitive plural in *-ium*, nominative and accusative plural of neuter in *-ia*.

Generally m. and f. forms are the same (the few exceptions are most unlikely to occur in local records).

e.g., *omnis*, m. f., *omne*, n.—all: for model see *tristis*, Kennedy, p. 22 (but ignore alternative accusative plural of m. and f.).

Often m., f., and n. forms are the same in nominative singular, e.g.:
presens, m., f., and n. (= present)—genitive *presentis*, so root is *present-*.

21

For model see *ingens*, Kennedy, p. 23.

A few exceptions are specially noted in Word List (e.g., *compos*, adj.—in possession of); these behave like the nouns.

NOTE. Sometimes adjectives (of any declension) may be used to take the place of nouns; the gender and number, together with context, will indicate how they should be translated, e.g.:

alii domini regis fideles—other faithful (subjects) of the lord King.

Sciant omnes—Know all (men).

PRACTICE

1. *Sciant omnes quod** (Know all [men] that . . .) *nos Willelmus Spence et Willelmus Blake capellani dedimus et hac presenti carta nostra confirmavimus Cristofero Teyt generoso et Alicie uxori eius omnia et singula messuagia que nuper habuimus ex dono et concessione Willelmi Hyl vicarii ecclesie pariochialis Sancti Michaelis.*

2. *Hec est* (is) *finalis concordia facta* (made) *in curia domini regis apud Westmonasterium coram Francisco North, Johanne Archer et Willelmo Ellys Justiciariis et aliis domini regis fidelibus tunc ibi presentibus, inter Ricardum Hall generosum, querentem, et Philippum Price et Elizabetham uxorem eius, deforciantes, de manerio de Tyseley.*

3. *Sciant presentes et futuri quod** (Know [men] present and future that . . .) *ego Thomas Picard dedi et hac presenti carta mea confirmavi Isabelle filie Simonis unum tenementum in Shepton vocatum Rudcroft cum terris et pratis adiacentibus, nuper in tenura Johannis atte Grene.*

4. *Noverint universi quod** (Know all [men] that . . .) *ego Ricardus Godwyne dedi Roberto Mennye et Willelmo Lane et heredibus et assignatis eorum omnia tenementa cum omnibus suis pertinenciis que nuper habui infra villam de Whithulle.*

5. *Sciant presentes et futuri quod** *Ego R. de Ryton, miles, dedi Johanni filio meo et heredibus suis masculis de corpore suo legitime procreatis omnes terras quas quondam Robertus filius Rogeri fratris mei tenuit in villa de Ryton.*

1. Know all [men] that we, W. S. and W. B., chaplains, have given and by this our present charter confirmed to C. T., gentleman, and to Alice his wife all and every messuage [lit. messuages, generally translated 'all and singular the messuages'] which we lately had from the gift and grant of W. H., vicar of the parish church of St. Michael.

* Special use of *quod* to mean 'that'—extremely common in medieval documents.

2. This is the final agreement made in the court of the lord King at Westminster before F. N., J. A., and W. E., Justices, and other faithful (subjects) of the lord King then there present, between R. H., gentleman, querent, and P. P. and E. his wife, deforciants, concerning the manor of T.

3. Know [men] present and future that I, T. P., have given and by this my present charter confirmed to I., daughter of Simon, one tenement in S., called Rudcroft with lands and meadows adjacent, lately in the tenure of John atte Grene.

4. Know all [men] that I, R. G., have given to R. M. and W. L. and their heirs and assigns all tenements with all their appurtenances which I lately had in the vill of W.

5. Know [men] present and future that I, R. de R., knight, have given to John my son and to his male heirs of his body lawfully begotten, all lands which the late R., son of my brother Roger, held in the vill of R.

II

Fourth and fifth declensions

Both contain nouns only.

1. Fourth declension is so like third as hardly to merit a separate category. The root always ends in *u* except for dative and ablative plural, where the *u* disappears, plus endings as follows:

	SINGULAR	PLURAL
N.	–*s*	–*s*
A.	–*m*	–*s*
G.	–*s*	–*um*
D.	–*i*	–*ibus*
A.	—	–*ibus*

Model: *gradus*, Kennedy, p. 17 (neuters are very unlikely to occur in local records); dative and ablative plural *gradibus*.

BUT for irregular word *domus*, 'house', see Kennedy, p. 18.

2. Fifth declension has a very small number of words. See model: *res*, Kennedy, p. 18. Again similarities with third declension will be noticed. The only words likely to occur in local records are:

res—thing
dies—day } both have singular and plural

fides—faith
meridies—midday; south } only in singular

Students will now find it helpful in practice to use the preliminary page of the Word List on 'How to determine declension of nouns and adjectives'.

PRACTICE

1. *Hec est finalis concordia facta in curia domini Regis apud Coventre die*★ *Lune proxima post festum Assumpcionis beate Marie, anno*★ *regni Regis*

★ *die, anno*: ablative used to express time at which, or during which, a thing happens.

anno . . . vicesimo—'in the twentieth year of the reign . . .' In dating by regnal

Henrici vicesimo, coram Roberto de Lexington, Olivero de Vallibus et Johanne de Hulecote, Justiciariis itinerantibus, et aliis domini Regis fidelibus tunc ibi presentibus, INTER *Robertum de Ware et Amiciam uxorem eius, petentes, et Hugonem de Brandon, tenentem, de triginta et sex acris terre cum pertinenciis in Wolvey in comitatu Warwici, unde placitum fuit* (has been) *inter eos in eadem curia.*

2. *Et pro hac remissione, quietaclamancia, fine et concordia, idem Hugo dedit predictis Roberto et Amicie quattuor marcas argenti.*

1. This is the final agreement made in the court of the lord King at Coventry on Monday ('day of the moon') next after the feast of the Assumption of Blessed Mary, in the twentieth year of the reign of King Henry, before Robert de L., Oliver de V., and John de H., Justices itinerant (Justices in Eyre), and other faithful (subjects) of the lord King then there present, BETWEEN R. de W. and Amice his wife, plaintiffs, and H. de B., defendant, concerning 36 acres of land with appurtenances in Wolvey in the county of Warwick, in respect whereof a plea has been (made) between them in the same court.

2. And for this remise, quitclaim, fine and agreement, the same Hugh has given (the past or perfect tense can be translated thus) to the aforesaid R. and A. four marks of silver.

---

year, the word *anno* and the number going with it are ALWAYS separated as in this example.

NOTE common expressions in deeds:

post conquestum, a conquestu—'after the conquest', 'from the conquest'.

pro redditu—'for a rent'.

pro summa pecunie pre manibus soluta—'for a sum of money paid beforehand'.

12

Participles, past and future, formation; use of future participle

1. The four key parts of a verb as given in dictionaries are:

Do (I give) present tense
Dare (to give) the infinitive
Dedi (I gave) past or perfect tense
Datum: this part, the supine, is not much used, but is given because two participles are formed from it:

(a) Past participle: by changing the *m* to *s*, *datus*, meaning 'given', or 'having been given', which then agrees with nouns, and declines like *predictus*: *datus, -a, -um*.

(b) Future participle: by changing the *m* to *rus*, *daturus* (*-a, -um*), meaning 'about to give'.

This process holds good for all types of verbs:

video, videre, vidi, visum—to see (an irregular second-conjugation verb); past part.: *visus, -a, -um*—seen, or, having been seen; future part.: *visurus, -a, -um*—about to see.

audio, audire, audivi, auditum—to hear (fourth conjugation); past part.: *auditus, -a, -um*—heard, having been heard; future part.: *auditurus, -a, -um*—about to hear.

2. The future participle is very common at the beginning of charters. (The uses of the past participle will be seen later.) An opening sentence might run:

Omnibus Christi fidelibus hoc presens scriptum visuris vel audituris Johannes Archer salutem in domino sempiternam.
Literally: 'To all the faithful of Christ about to see or about to hear this present writing, J. A. (gives) eternal greeting in the Lord.' Note *visuris* and *audituris* agreeing with *fidelibus*, and the omission of the verb.

PRACTICE

1. *Notum sit* (be it known) *omnibus hoc presens scriptum visuris vel*

26

audituris quod (that) *ego dominus Petrus de Teynton dedi et hoc presenti scripto meo confirmavi Roberto de Bley et Reynilde uxori sue pro serviciis suis et centum solidis argenti, unum messuagium et dimidiam virgatam terre mee, illud messuagium videlicet et illam dimidiam virgatam terre quam terram et quod messuagium Simo Ellys aliquando tenuit in villa de Teynton cum pertinenciis suis, et cum omnibus pratis pasturis et viis ad predictum messuagium et terram pertinentibus* ('pertaining to' agreeing with *pratis, pasturis, viis*).

2. *Sciant presentes et futuri quod ego Ida Priorissa de Aston assensu et consensu sororum domus nostre dedi . . . Rogero de Wyche et uxori sue ad totam vitam eorum unum messuagium, illud scilicet quod Sarra tenuit cum omnibus pertinenciis et unum pratum cum buttis in campo de Aston et quattuordecim seliones terre arrabilis que iacent in eodem campo.*

1. Be it known to all about to see or hear* this present writing that I lord P. de T. have given and by this my present charter confirmed to R. de B. and to R. his wife for their services and a hundred shillings of silver, one messuage and a half virgate of my land (that messuage namely and that half virgate of land which land and which messuage Simon E. at some time held), in the vill of T., with their appurtenances and with all meadows pastures and ways pertaining to the aforesaid messuage and land.

2. Know (men) present and future that I, Ida, Prioress of Aston with the assent and consent of the sisters of our house, have given to R. de W. and his wife for their whole life, one messuage, that, namely, which Sarah held, with all appurtenances and one meadow with butts in the field of A. and fourteen selions of arable land which lie in the same field.

* i.e., illiterates.

NOTE expression in the dating of deeds:
Datum apud Wolvey—'given at Wolvey'.

13

Future tense; *Ego*

1. Future tense

For models see Kennedy, pp. 42, 44, 46, 48, where it is called 'future simple'.

NOTE. First and second conjugation futures are the same, except for the characteristic vowel: *a* in the first, *e* in the second.

So, *warantizabo*—I will warrant (*warantizo*, first conjugation)
habebo—I shall have (*habeo*, second conjugation)

Third and fourth conjugations are alike, except that in fourth, the root always ends in *i*.

So, *defendam*—I will defend (*defendo*, third conjugation)
audiam—I shall hear (*audio*, fourth conjugation)

2. See also Kennedy, p. 30, declension of *ego*. Medieval Latin often has *michi* for *mihi*.

PRACTICE

1. *Pateat* (be it manifest) *universis quod ego Nicholas de Wodeton dedi . . . Willelmo Mannys pro summa pecunie quam mihi pre manibus dedit unum messuagium duos* (two) *gardinos et totam terram illam quam tenui apud Wodeton in manerio de Honesworth.*

2. *Et ego vero dictus Nicholas et heredes mei omnia predicta tenementa dicto Willelmo heredibus suis vel suis assignatis pro predicto redditu sex denariorum contra omnes homines et feminas warantizabimus acquietabimus et defendemus imperpetuum.*

3. *Et ego Hugo et heredes mei predictam virgatam terre cum tofto et crofto et omnibus pertinenciis suis dicto Roberto et heredibus suis contra omnes gentes warantizabimus imperpetuum, et pro hac donatione concessione et warantia dedit michi dictus Robertus quadraginta solidos argenti.*

1. Be it manifest to all that I Nicholas de W. have given . . . to W. M., for a sum of money which he gave to me beforehand, one

messuage, two gardens and all that land which I held at W. in the manor of H.

2. And truly I the said N. and my heirs will warrant, acquit and defend forever all the aforesaid tenements to the said W., his heirs or his assigns, against all men and women, in return for (*pro*) the aforesaid rent of six pence.

3. And I, H., and my heirs will warrant against all people forever the aforesaid virgate of land with toft and croft and all its appurtenances to the said R. and his heirs, and for this gift, grant and warrant the said R. has given me (lit., to me) 40 shillings of silver.

14

Past (perfect) and future perfect

---

1. Formation

The third part of a verb given in a dictionary is the past (perfect):

confirmo, -are, -avi, -atum (1st conjug.)—to confirm
do, dare, dedi,* *datum* (1st)—to give
habeo, -ere, habui, habitum (2nd)—to have
concedo, -ere, -cessi,* *-cessum* (3rd)—to grant
audio, -ire, -ivi, -itum (4th)—to hear

Two irregular verbs:

obeo, -ire, obii, obitum (4th)—to die
volo, velle, volui (not classed as any conjug.)—to wish, to want, to intend, etc.

The past (perfect) root of all verbs is revealed by removing the final *i*:

So,	*confirmav–*	*ded–*	*habu–*	*concess–*
	audiv–	*obi–*	*volu–*	

The past (perfect) endings (see Chapter 5) are then added to give the full tense, e.g.:

concessi	I granted	*concessimus*	we granted
concessisti	you granted	*concessistis*	you granted
concessit	he, she, it, granted	*concesserunt*†	they granted

Future perfect is formed by adding:

–ero	*–erimus*
–eris	*–eritis*
–erit	*–erint*†

to the past (perfect) root, e.g.:

voluero (I shall have wished), etc.
obiero (I shall have died), etc.

* NOTE irregular root in past.
† BEWARE of confusing third person plural of past and future perfect.

30

2. Use of future perfect

The future (simple): I shall do

Future perfect: I shall have done, e.g., 'I shall have finished the book by tonight'; i.e., by tonight the reading will be finished, but at the moment of speaking the reading is in the future, so both future and past are involved.

Typical uses in deeds:

(a) 'Greetings to those to whom this charter shall have come' (i.e., to people in the future, into whose hands the deed has come, so past and future together).

(b) 'I leave my land to my son after my death unless he shall have died before then.'

(c) 'The property is to be held by him or his heirs or by anyone to whom he shall have decided to sell or bequeath it.'

PRACTICE

1. *Omnibus Christi fidelibus ad quos presentes littere pervenerint Henricus de Broughton capellanus salutem in domino sempiternam. Ego prefatus Henricus remisi* (see *remitto*) *Alicie relicte Willelmi Haighe pro me et heredibus meis imperpetuum totum ius quod habeo vel in futurum habebo in omnibus illis messuagiis, terris, tenementis, redditibus et serviciis cum suis pertinenciis, que nuper habui conjunctim cum Roberto Haighe in comitatu Lancastrie.*

2. *Et si contingat* (and if it should·happen) *quod predictus Robertus sine herede masculo de corpore suo legitime procreato obierit, tunc volo et concedo quod predicte terre Ricardo, fratri Roberti predicti, remaneant* (should remain).

3. *In cuius rei testimonium sigillum meum hoc scripto apposui* (see *appono*). *Datum decimo die Septembris, anno regni Regis Henrici sexti post conquestum Anglie vicesimo.*

1. To all Christ's faithful to whom the present letters shall have come, H. de B., chaplain, (gives) eternal greeting in the Lord. I the aforesaid H. have remised to Alice widow of W. H., on behalf of myself and my heirs forever, all the right which I have or in future shall have in all those messuages, lands, tenements, rents and services with their appurtenances, which I lately had jointly with R. H. in the county of Lancaster.

2. And if it should happen that the aforesaid R. shall have died without male heir of his body lawfully begotten, then I will and grant that

the aforesaid lands should remain to Richard brother of the aforesaid Robert.

3. In testimony of which* I have affixed my seal to this writing. Given on the 10th day of September, in the 20th year (*anno vicesimo*) of the reign of King Henry the Sixth after the conquest.

* Literally, 'of which thing'.

NOTE the use of the future perfect in these typical phrases:

... *concessi* ... *reversionem cuiusdam messuagii* ... *quando acciderit*—I have granted ... the reversion of a certain messuage ... when it falls due (lit. shall have fallen due)

licebit eis distringere ... *donec plenarie eis satisfactum fuerit de arreragiis redditus*—it shall. be allowed to them to distrain ... until satisfaction shall have been fully made to them for the arrears of rent.

15

Present and past participles; ablative absolute

1. Present and past participles

   (a) Present participle—the formation will be clear from these examples:

   1st conjugation—*dans*, (genitive) *dantis*—giving (from *do*)
   2nd conjugation—*iacens*, (genitive) *iacentis*—lying (from *iaceo*)
   3rd conjugation—*ducens*, (genitive) *ducentis*—leading (from *duco*)
   4th conjugation—*serviens*, (genitive) *servientis*—serving (from *servio*)

   All agree like adjectives and decline like *ingens* (Kennedy, p. 23), but often ablative singular ends in -*e*.

   Some uses
   via ducens ad villam—a road leading to the vill.
   dedi terras iacentes in illa parochia—I gave lands lying in that parish.
   omnia aisiamenta dicto tenemento spectantia—all easements belonging to the said tenement (from *specto*—to belong to, etc.).

   (b) Past participle—for formation see Chapter 12.

   Some uses
   per servicia inde debita et de iure consueta—by the services thence owed and by right accustomed.
   messuagium vocatum Grenesplace—a messuage called Grenesplace.
   et hac presenti carta nostra indentata confirmavimus—and by this our present indented charter we have confirmed . . .

   NOTE. Many participles, past and present, will be found individually entered in the Word List at the end of the book.

2. ABLATIVE ABSOLUTE CONSTRUCTION

   (a) Sometimes a phrase containing a participle is, as it were, independent of the main part of the sentence, and is described as 'absolute', the words in it not being linked with the main part: e.g., <u>All things being equal</u>, I shall come tomorrow.
   ('absolute')

BUT, <u>Being an honest man</u>, John returned the purse.
(not 'absolute')

Here the word 'being' goes with 'John', in the main part of the sentence, so the phrase is not 'absolute'.

> The matter having been settled in committee ('absolute'), there is nothing more to say.

(b) In Latin it is a trick of language to put the key words of an absolute phrase into the ablative case, without implying its usual meaning of 'by, with, from'.

In the present:

I have given, granted, and by this my charter confirmed, to Richard, one virgate of land . . . these being witnesses, John, Robert son of William, Henry, and many others ('absolute': the phrase from 'these' to the end).

Dedi, concessi, etc. . . . . hiis testibus, Johanne, Roberto filio Willelmi, Henrico, et multis aliis.

NOTE. 1. 'being' is always omitted in Latin, as the verb 'to be' lacks this participle.

2. *Johanne, Roberto filio, Henrico, . . . multis aliis* are all ablative, because they stand beside *hiis testibus* to make its meaning clear (see Chapter 4, Practice I).

3. This witnessing clause occurs in nearly all deeds.

In the past:

A proclamation having been made ('absolute'), the lands are handed over to Hugh.

Proclamatione facta, terre Hugoni dimittuntur.

Facta—past participle (of *facio, facere, feci, factum*, to do or make), ablative, agreeing with *proclamatione*.

EXAMPLES OF ABLATIVE ABSOLUTE

1. *Hoc contra omnes homines Johanni imperpetuum warantizabimus pro predicto servicio, <u>salvo forinseco servicio domini regis</u>.*

We shall warrant this to John against all men forever, for the aforesaid service, saving foreign service of the lord king.

NOTE. *Salvus, -a, -um*, adj.—safe. Literally, 'foreign service of the lord king [being] safe', i.e., left untouched, left out, excepted.

2. *Dedi . . . tenementum cum omnibus pertinentiis, <u>excepto horreo</u>.*

I gave . . . a tenement with all appurtenances, excepting the barn. Literally, 'the barn having been taken out' or 'excepted'; *excepto*—past participle of *excipio, excipere, excepi, exceptum*, to take out.

PRACTICE

1. *Hec est finalis concordia facta in curia domini regis apud Westmonasterium a die Pasche in quindecim dies, anno regni regis Johannis primo.* Note unusual expression indicating date, often used in fines, *a die . . . in dies*— meaning 'on the 15th day after Easter', reckoned inclusively. But in studying actual fines, see C. R. Cheney, *Handbook of Dates* (London, 1955), p. 65, for Law Terms.

2. *Dedi . . . terram scituatum, iacentem et existentem in Escott in dicto comitatu, ac modo vel nuper in tenura sive occupacione Rogeri Davye, et omnes meas domos et terras quascumque* (whatsoever) *in manerio de Barsell cum omnibus libertatibus eisdem tenementis pertinentibus vel spectantibus.*

3. . . . *reddendo* (rendering) *inde annuatim mihi et heredibus meis tres solidos argenti ad quattuor anni terminos, scilicet ad festum Sancti Andree novem denarios, ad festum beate Marie in Martio novem denarios, ad festum Sancti Johannis Baptiste novem denarios, ad festum Sancti Michaelis novem denarios, pro omni servicio et demanda mihi vel heredibus meis pertinenti, salvo servicio forinseco.*

4. *Pateat per presentes quod ego Johannes de Hales ordinavi et loco meo constitui Gilbertum de Wyke attornatum meum . . . dans eidem plenam potestatem nomine meo facere* (to act) *in his premissis. . . .*

5. *Proclamacione inde facta et nullo prohibenti, predicte ix acre terre arrabilis iacentes in villa supranominata predicto Henrico per senescallum dimittuntur* (are demised).

1. This is the final agreement made in the court of the lord king at Westminster fifteen days from Easter day, in the first year of the reign of King John.

2. I gave . . . land situated, lying and existing in Escott in the said county, and now or recently in the tenure or occupation of R. D., and all my houses and lands whatsoever in the manor of Barsell with all liberties pertaining or belonging to the same tenements (distinguish *pertinentibus*, pres. part., from *pertinenciis*, appurtenances).

3. . . . rendering thence annually to me and my heirs 3 shillings of silver at the 4 terms of the year, namely at the feast of St. Andrew 9*d*, at the feast of Blessed Mary in March, 9*d*, at the feast of St. John the

Baptist, 9*d*, at the feast of St. Michael, 9*d*, for all service and claim belonging to me or my heirs, saving foreign service.

4. Be it manifest by (these) presents that I, J. de H., have appointed and set up in my place G. de W. (as) my attorney . . . giving to the same, full power to act in my name in these premises. . . .

5. A proclamation having then been made and no one forbidding (it), the aforesaid 9 acres of arable land lying in the above-named vill, are demised to the aforesaid H. by the steward.

16

Comparison of adjectives and adverbs; verb 'to be'; court rolls

1. Comparison of adjectives and adverbs:

The following two adjectives show the most common and straight-forward formation of the comparative and superlative.

ADJECTIVES	COMPARATIVE		SUPERLATIVE
	M. F.	N.	
latus, -a, -um	*latior*	*latius*	*latissimus, -a, -um*
wide	wider		widest
brevis, -e	*brevior*	*brevius*	*brevissimus, -a, -um*
short	shorter		shortest

A small number of adjectives ending in *-er* have the superlative ending in *-errimus*.

eger, egra, egrum	*egrior*	*egrius*	*egerrimus, -a, -um*
ill	more ill		most ill

The following six have the superlative ending in *-illimus*: *facilis, difficilis, similis, dissimilis, gracilis, humilis.*

facilis, -e	*facilior*	*facilius*	*facillimus, -a, -um*
easy	easier		easiest

The comparative declines like third-declension nouns (Kennedy, p. 24, §49), the superlative like *predictus, -a, -um*. The handful of irregular words (e.g., *bonus*—good, *melior*—better, *optimus*—best) are entered individually in the Word List. Local historians are not likely to meet comparatives or superlatives very frequently.

ADVERBS	COMPARATIVE	SUPERLATIVE
late	*latius*	*latissime*
widely	more widely	most widely
breviter	*brevius*	*brevissime*
shortly	more shortly	most shortly

ADVERBS	COMPARATIVE	SUPERLATIVE
facile	*facilius*	*facillime*
easily	more easily	most easily

These do not, of course, decline. The formation of an adverb corresponding to a given adjective is not always straightforward, but adverbs are individually listed in dictionaries and word lists, and the local historian need not trouble about the rules. The formation of comparative and superlative of adverbs is stereotyped as above, and will be obvious.

2. The verb 'to be' (Kennedy, p. 40). The present and past (perfect) are the most likely to be encountered (notice that the perfect is regular in its formation based on the perfect root *fu-*). It is advisable to use Kennedy for reference rather than attempt to learn the full conjugation at this stage.

MANOR AND BOROUGH COURT ROLLS

Practice material from these will be given from now on. The grammar is often rather sketchy; the clerks in describing everyday events brought up in the courts often wrote Latin close to English idiom, and ignored many of the rules. A study of printed Court Rolls with English translations will familiarize the student with the type of subject-matter and the manner of presenting it. In examples given here divergences from standard practice will be explained.

PRACTICE

1. *Walterus filius Walteri, et Thomas Fallas venerunt in campo vocato Shroley, baculos in manibus portantes, ubi dictus Hugo fuit in pace domini ville, et iniuste eum insultaverunt.*

2. *Simo venit in plena curia et petivit a Petro XXs pro bidentibus sibi* (to him) *venditis. Idem Petrus presens negavit omnia de verbo ad verbum, et inde est ad legem cum VI manu.**

3. *Robertus, garcio dicti Edwardi, ivit* (from *eo*) *cum averiis extra villam in alta via que est inter Hetherifurlong et Langefurlong, ducens†* ad pasturam *suam.*

4. *Necnon predicto Johanni concessimus quacumque septimana durante vita eiusdem Johannis tres lagenas et dimidiam cervisie conventualis, ac quolibet*

---

* *cum VI manu*—translate 'six-handed', i.e., with five compurgators; one would expect *manibus*, plural, but this is the regular phrase.

† *ducens* agrees with *que*; the idiom is English rather than Latin.

anno unam carecturam feni et quattuor carecturas ligni annuatim pro seculari servicio, et ad Natale domini unum habitum sicut honestiores servientes ibidem habere usitati sunt, cum clausa districcionis in omnibus terris et tenementis nostris, prout plenius apparet in litteris patentibus nostris.

5. *Item camerarii petunt* (seek) *allocacionem de xv⁸ pro reparatione de le Bullringe.*

1. Walter son of Walter and Thomas Fallas came into the field called Shroley carrying sticks in their hands, where the said Hugh was in the peace of the lord of the vill, and they unjustly assaulted him.

2. Simon came in full court and sought 20s. from Peter for sheep sold to him. The same Peter (being) present, denied all, word for word (lit., from word to word), and thereupon is at law six-handed.

3. Robert, the boy of the said Edward, came with beasts out of the vill on to the high road which is between Hetherifurlong and Lange-furlong, leading to his pasture.

4. And we have granted to the aforesaid John each week during the life (note ablative absolute, lit., the life lasting) of the same John, $3\frac{1}{2}$ gallons of conventual ale, and each year one cart-load of hay and 4 cart-loads of wood annually for secular service, and at Christmas (the birthday of the Lord), one habit such as the more respectable servants there are accustomed to have, with a clause of distraint on all our lands and tenements, as more fully appears in our letters patent.

5. Likewise the chamberlains seek an allowance of 15s for the repair of the Bullring.

17

Passive verbs; deponents; semi-deponents

1. Passive verbs

The verbs met so far have been active, i.e., they have done the action, e.g.:

They call that land Blackheath. *Illam terram Blackheath vocant.*

In the case of a passive verb, its subject has the action done to it, e.g.:

That land is called Blackheath. *Illa terra Blackheath vocatur.*

NOTE. The Latin verb takes a special form. For model passives, see Kennedy, pp. 50, 52, 54, 56.

The second person, singular and plural, is rare in local records, except for certain types of ecclesiastical documents.

Formation of first and third persons, in present, imperfect, future simple, in all conjugations:

(*a*) First person, singular and plural, ends in -*r*, i.e., *r* is added to the active when it ends in a vowel:

1st conjug.	*voco*—I call	*vocabo*—I shall call
	vocor—I am called	*vocabor*—I shall be called
2nd conjug.	*teneo*—I hold	*tenebo*—I shall hold
	teneor—I am held	*tenebor*—I shall be held
3rd conjug.	*peto*—I seek	
	petor—I am sought	
4th conjug.	*audio*—I hear	
	audior—I am heard	

When active ends in a consonant, this is changed to *r*, e.g.:

vocamus—we call   *vocabimus*—we shall call
vocamur—we are called   *vocabimur*—we shall be called
vocabam—I was calling
vocabar—I was being called
petam—I shall seek
petar—I shall be sought   . . . and so on.

(b) Third person, singular and plural, ends in *-ur*, which is simply added to the active forms, e.g.:

vocat—he, she, it calls   *vocant*—they call
vocatur—he, she, it is called   *vocantur*—they are called

tenet—he, etc., holds
tenetur—he, etc., is held

and so on for future and imperfect, all conjugations.

(c) Formation of past perfect, future perfect, pluperfect, passive (all conjugations): the past participle plus parts of the verb 'to be'.

<table>
<tr><td>Past perfect</td><td>*vocatus sum*—I was called (or, I have been called)</td></tr>
<tr><td>Future perfect</td><td>*vocatus ero*—I shall have been called</td></tr>
<tr><td>Pluperfect</td><td>*vocatus eram* (sometimes *fui*, perfect of verb 'to be', is used here)—I had been called</td></tr>
</table>

NOTE (a). The participle resembles an adjective, so agrees with the subject of the verb in number and gender:

Illud messuagium vocatum est Scarcroft.
That messuage was called Scarcroft.

Ille terre vocate sunt Longefurlong.
Those lands were called Longefurlong.

NOTE (b). These tenses are often used loosely in court rolls, where the verb 'to be' is generally translated literally in the following type of phrases:

Presentatum est quod Ricardus fodivit pratum.
It is presented that Richard has dug up the meadow.

Preceptum est distringere Walterum pro defalta.
It is ordered to distrain Walter for default.

Proceedings in Manor Courts are written down at the time in the present tense, so that the context indicates the above translation rather than 'was presented', 'was ordered'.

In fact, in all medieval Latin there is a tendency for the past participle to be regarded simply as an adjective, and for the verb 'to be' in these compound passive tenses to be translated literally.

2. Deponent verbs

A limited number of verbs (followed in Word List by abbreviation 'depon.') exist only in the passive form, but have an active meaning, i.e., they 'lay down' (*depono*—to lay down) their passive meaning, e.g.: *queror*—I complain; *ingredior*—I enter.

They have present participles formed like ordinary verbs, e.g., *querens, querentis*—complaining. Their past participles are active in meaning, e.g., *questus, -a, -um*—having complained.

3. Semi-deponents

Only two of these are likely to be met:

> *gaudeo, gaudere, gavisus sum*—to enjoy.
> *soleo, solere, solitus sum*—to be accustomed.

It will be seen that *only the perfect* (and tenses based on it) is of passive form (and active meaning). A further complication here is that the past participles *gavisus* and *solitus may* be used in a passive way, meaning 'enjoyed' and 'accustomed':

e.g., *cum omnibus pertinenciis vel libertatibus inde usitatis, occupatis sive gavisis.*
> 'with all appurtenances or liberties thereof used, occupied or enjoyed' (the context makes the meaning clear).

PRACTICE

1. *Alicie filie Ricardi, quia nihil habet, misericordia remittitur, et quieta est.*

2. *Adam ingressus est* (from *ingredior*, deponent) *in unam acram terre de feodo domini, ideo preceptum est eum distringere.*

3. *Terra que fuit in manu Sibille capitur in manu domini quia heres de plena etate est, et predicta Sibilla dotatur de tercia parte.*

4. *Loquela tangens Hugonem de auxilio vocato Beupleys ponitur in respectum ad proximam curiam eo quod* [lit., from this (cause), that = because] *Simo contradicit plegium dicti Hugonis.*

5. *Ricardus et Christina uxor eius attachiati sunt quod inventi fuerunt in blado domini.*

6. *Stephanus queritur versus Ricardum de placito debiti iiii solidorum.*

7. *Sciant omnes quod ego Thomas Clare de Ware teneor et obligatus sum Nicholao Poole de Stanes in quadraginta libris bone et legalis monete Anglie.*

8. *Hoc Inventorium fuit attestatum et probatum; Curia Baronis tenta apud Bromley octavo die Maii . . . per sacramentum Agnetis Bullock executricis ultimi vellei et testamenti Ricardi Bullock, coram Henrico Worthe, Senescallo curie predicte.*

9. *Postea respectuantur eisdem camerariis iii^s x^d in panello supra de defectu redditus. Et sic debent claro vi^{li} x^s . . . .*

10. *Ballivi ville presentant quod Willelmus Russell (iij^d) Thomas Bury*

(iij^d) et Ricardus Higges (iij^d) mercatores panni, vocati drapers, stant extra communes stallas mercatorum diebus fororum, contra antiquam consuetudinem ville, et in prejudicium jurum et libertatum ville predicte.

1. To Alice daughter of Richard mercy is remitted, because she has nothing, and she is quit.

2. Adam has entered (this is a permissible way of translating past perfect) into one acre of land of the lord's fee, therefore it is ordered to distrain him.

3. The land which was in the hands (lit., hand) of Sybil is taken into the lord's hands because the heir is of full age, and the aforesaid S. is dowered of the third part.

4. The action touching Hugh concerning the aid called 'Beupleys' is adjourned (lit., placed in respite) to the next court because Simon refuses (to be) the pledge of the said Hugh.

5. Richard and Christine his wife were attached because they had been found in the lord's corn. (Some translators might regard both *attachiati* and *inventi* as adjectives rather than participles and render it 'are attached . . . were found'.)

6. Stephen complains against Richard concerning a plea of debt for (lit., of) four shillings.

7. Know all (men) that I Thomas Clare of Ware am held and am bound (*obligatus* used simply as adjective, so translate *sum* as present tense, as is indicated by *teneor*, the two verbs always being parallel in bonds) to Nicholas Poole of Stanes in 40 pounds of good and lawful money of England.

8. This Inventory was attested and proved: Court Baron (lit., of the Baron) held at B. on the 8th day of May . . . by the oath of Agnes Bullock, executrix of the last will and testament of Richard Bullock, before Henry Worthe, Steward of the aforesaid court.

9. Next, 3s 4d in the above list of default of rent is (lit., are) respited to the same chamberlains. And thus they owe £6. 10s net. . . .

10. The bailiffs of the town present that Wm. Russell (3d), Thos. Bury (3d) and Rich. Higges (3d), cloth-merchants, called drapers, stand outside the common stalls of the merchants (i.e., the market-stalls) on market-days, contrary to the ancient custom of the town, and in prejudice of the rights and liberties of the aforesaid town.

18

Infinitives; accusative and infinitive construction

Infinitives

1. Active, (*a*) present: this is given in dictionaries, generally abbreviated, as follows.

> *obligo, -are, -avi, -atum* (1)—to bind, i.e., *obligare*
> *teneo, -ere, -ui, tentum* (2)—to hold, i.e., *tenere*
> *concedo, -ere, -cessi, -cessum* (3)—to grant, i.e., *concedere*
> *audio, -ire, -ivi, -itum* (4)—to hear, i.e., *audire*

> (*b*) past (or perfect): take the perfect root and add *-isse*.

> | | |
> |---|---|
> | *obligav-isse* | to have bound |
> | *tenu-isse* | to have held |
> | *concess-isse* | to have granted |
> | *audiv-isse* | to have heard |

NOTE. Where the perfect root ends in *v* the perfect infinitive is often shortened, omitting *vi*: e.g., *obligasse, audisse*; or *v* only: e.g., *audiisse*. The perfect itself is often similarly shortened: e.g., *audii*—I heard, *petii*—I sought, though not in first conjugation.

> (*c*) future: the future participle with *esse* (present infinitive of verb 'to be').

> | | |
> |---|---|
> | *obligaturus esse* | to be about to bind |
> | *tenturus esse* | to be about to hold |
> | *concessurus esse* | to be about to grant |
> | *auditurus esse* | to be about to hear |

NOTE. The future participle declines like *predictus* and agrees with the subject of the verb; for formation, see Chapter 12.

2. Passive, (*a*) present: change the final *e* of the present infinitive active to *i*.

> | | |
> |---|---|
> | *obligari* | to be bound |
> | *teneri* | to be held |
> | *audiri* | to be heard |

44

BUT NOTE. Third conjugation is a short form, made by changing the first *e* of the present infinitive to *i*: *concedi*—to be granted.

> (b) past (or perfect): the past participle with *esse*.
>
> | | |
> |---|---|
> | *obligatus esse* | to have been bound |
> | *tentus esse* | to have been held |
> | *concessus esse* | to have been granted |
> | *auditus esse* | to have been heard |

NOTE. The past participle declines like *predictus* and agrees with the subject of the verb.

> (c) future: the past participle with *fore*, the future infinitive of the verb 'to be', which means 'about to be'.
>
> | | |
> |---|---|
> | *obligatus fore* | to be about to be bound |
> | *tentus fore* | to be about to be held |
> | *concessus fore* | to be about to be granted |
> | *auditus fore* | to be about to be heard |

NOTES. (a) The past participle declines as usual.
(b) The future infinitives will not be found often in local records.
(c) The infinitives of deponents follow the above scheme of passive infinitives.

ACCUSATIVE AND INFINITIVE CONSTRUCTION

Consider the two ways of saying the same thing in English:

1. I know that he is just.
2. I know him to be just.

The second has an accusative (him) and an infinitive (to be); this is therefore called an accusative and infinitive construction.

Both ways are used in Latin:

1. *Scio quod Henricus justus est*—I know that Henry is just.
2. *Scio Henricum justum esse*—I know Henry to be just. (NOTE: *iustum* is accusative to agree with *Henricum*.)

The accusative and infinitive construction is common in deeds, e.g.:

Notum sit   me prefatum Henricum   remisisse   totum ius meum
Be it known   me the aforesaid H.   to have remised   all my right
in illis terris.
in those lands.

Translate: 'Be it known that I the aforesaid H. have remised. . . .'
(NOTE: *remisisse* = perfect infinitive of *remitto*.)

PRACTICE

1. *Noveritis* (know ye) *me Matildam in pura viduetate mea concessisse, relaxasse* (full form *relaxavisse*) *et omnino quietumclamasse* (for *quietumclamavisse*) *Ade filio meo et heredibus suis totum ius meum vel clamium quod habui nomine dotis in omnibus terris et tenementis quibuscumque,* que sunt dicti Ade filii mei die confeccionis huius scripti una cum homagio et servicio Ade filio Rogeri de Turton et heredum suorum in ville de Elsbye.

2. *Predicti Adam et Agnes uxor eius recognoverunt predicta tenementa cum pertinenciis esse ius ipsius Willelmi.*

3. *Noverint universi* (Know all men) *per presentes nos Carolum Field et Edwardum Baker teneri et firmiter obligari Ricardo Stocks in quinquaginta libris bone et legalis monete Anglie.*

4. *Et ego predictus Simon Warde fateor me contentatum et pacatum fore et in et pro summa ducentarum librarum bone et legalis monete Anglie michi per Ricardum Judd de Colshull pre manibus soluta.*

1. Know ye that I Matilda in my pure widowhood have granted, released and entirely quitclaimed (lit., me M. to have granted, etc.) to Adam my son and his heirs all my right or claim which I had in the name of dower in all lands and tenements whatsoever, which are (in the possession) of Adam my son on the day of completion of this writing, along with the homage and service to Adam (my) son of Roger de T. and of his heirs in the vill of E.

2. The aforesaid Adam and Agnes his wife acknowledged the aforesaid tenements with appurtenances to be the right of William himself (or, the same William).

3. Know all men by (these) presents that we Charles Field and Edward Baker are held and firmly bound (lit., us . . . to be held, etc.) to Richard Stocks in fifty pounds of good and lawful money of England.

4. And I the aforesaid Simon Warde confess that I shall be content and paid (lit., me . . . to be about to be content . . .) both in and for the sum of £200 of good and lawful money of England paid (*soluta*) to me beforehand by Richard Judd of C.

* See *quicumque* in Word List.

19

The subjunctive: formation and uses (1)

---

1. Formation: Actives—see Kennedy, pp. 43, 45, 47, 49.
Passives—Kennedy, pp. 51, 53, 55, 57.

(a) Present active: the characteristic vowel is *a*.

2nd conjugation—*habeam, habeas, habeat, habeamus, habeatis, habeant*
3rd   ,,   —*distringam, distringas*, etc.
4th   ,,   —*sciam, scias*, etc.

NOTE. First conjugation has the vowel *e* to distinguish it from the present indicative (tenses met so far have been straightforward statements of fact, and are described grammatically as 'indicative'; the meanings of the subjunctive will be shown later).

1st conjugation—*vocem, voces, vocet, vocemus, vocetis, vocent*

(b) Imperfect active: add the endings -*m*, -*s*, -*t*, -*mus*, -*tis*, -*nt* to the present infinitive.

1st conjugation—*vocarem, vocares*, etc.
2nd   ,,   —*haberem*, etc.
3rd   ,,   —*distringerem*, etc.
4th   ,,   —*scirem*, etc.

(c) Present and imperfect passive: these are formed from the actives on the principle described in Chapter 17.

(d) Perfect active: to the perfect root add -*erim*, -*eris*, -*erit*, -*erimus*, -*erint*.

1st conjugation—*vocaverim*, etc.
2nd   ,,   —*habuerim*, etc.
3rd   ,,   —*distrinxerim*, etc.
4th   ,,   —*sciverim*, etc.

(e) Pluperfect active: to the perfect infinitive add -*m*, -*s*, -*t*, -*mus*, -*tis*, -*nt*.

1st conjugation—*vocavissem, vocavisses*, etc.
2nd   ,,   —*habuissem*, etc.

3rd conjugation—*distrinxissem*, etc.
4th   „   —*scivissem*, etc.

(*f*) Perfect and pluperfect passives:

The past participle with the present subjective of the verb 'to be' (Kennedy, p. 41) gives the perfect subjunctive passive: *vocatus sim, sis, sit, vocati simus, sitis, sint.*

The past participle with imperfect subjunctive of verb 'to be' (Kennedy, p. 41) gives the imperfect subjunctive passive: *vocatus essem,* etc.

NOTE. The *present* subjunctive is the one most often met with.

2. Uses.

(*a*) To express a command, proclamation or wish:

e.g., *Vivat rex!*—May the king live! (i.e., 'Long live the king!'). This appears on royal charters, etc., with the royal portrait. *Vivat* is present subjunctive, third conjugation.

This kind of subjunctive is used in the openings of deeds:

e.g., *Sciant presentes et futuri . . .*—Know (men) present and future . . .

Sciatis quod . . .—Know ye that . . .

(*Sciant* and *sciatis*—present subjunctive, fourth conjugation)

Notum sit tam presentibus quam futuris quod . . .
Be it known to (men) both present and future that . . .

(*Sit*—present subjunctive of *esse*, to be)

(*b*) For other uses of subjunctive, see Chapter 20.

PRACTICE

(subjunctives underlined)

1. *Custumarii presentant quod Johannes vendidit tres acras terre sue Waltero nativo, ideo predicta terra capiatur in manu domini quousque dictus Walterus finem fecerit* (future perfect of *facio*—to do or make).

2. *. . . et post decessum predicti Ricardi omnia tenementa predicta Johanni predicto integre revertantur* (deponent).

3. *Juratores presentant quod Robertus et Ricardus braciaverunt et fregerun, assisam, ideo attachientur.*

4. *Noverint universi per presentes quod ego Ricardus le Deistere dedi,*

concessi, et hac presenti carta mea confirmavi Willelmo de Wytewell unum messuagium in Wikey.

5. *Pateat universis per presentes quod ego Simon le Especer de London ordinavi et loco meo constitui dilectum mihi in Christo Thomas de Boyden attornatum meum.*

6. *Tunc bene <u>liceat</u> predicto Johanni et heredibus et assignatis suis <u>ingredi</u>* (deponent infinitive, third conjugation) *et terram predictam retinere.*

NOTES. (a) *Capio, facio,* and *ingredior* (and verbs derived from them, e.g., *recipio, incipio, conficio,* etc.) are of mixed third and fourth conjugation (see Kennedy, p. 61).

(b) *Noverint* is perfect subjunctive of *nosco, -ere, novi, notum* (3). The present (and future) tenses of this mean 'to get to know', therefore the past tenses are used to mean 'to know'. Hence perfect subjunctive here, where normally present subjunctive of another verb would be used.

(c) *Pateat* and *liceat*—see Word List.

1. The customary tenants present that J. has sold three acres of his land to Walter the villein, therefore <u>let the aforesaid land be taken</u> into the hands (lit., hand) of the lord until the said W. <u>shall have made fine</u> (i.e., paid fine).

2. ... and after the death of the aforesaid R. <u>let</u> all the aforesaid tenements <u>revert</u> wholly to the aforesaid J.

3. The jurors present that R. and R. have brewed and have broken the assize, therefore <u>let them be attached.</u>

4. <u>Know all (men)</u> (or, <u>let all men know</u>) by (these) presents that I, R. le D., have given, granted and by this my present charter confirmed to W. de W. one messuage in W.

5. <u>Let it be known</u> to all (men) by (these) presents that I, S. le E. of London, have appointed and set up in my place as my attorney T. de B., beloved to me in Christ.

6. Then <u>let it be truly lawful</u> for the aforesaid J. and his heirs and assigns to enter and to retain the aforesaid land.

20

Uses of the subjunctive (2)

1. A further use after orders or commands is very common in court rolls:

It is ordered that Roger <u>should be distrained</u>.

Preceptum est ut (or *quod*) *Rogerus <u>distringatur</u>* (present subjective passive).

NOTES. (a) *preceptum est* translated as present: see Chapter 17, note (b).

(b) A negative command or prohibition may be introduced by *ne*—that . . . not:

Preceptum est ne tenentes exitus habeant ex opposito bladi domini.
It is ordered <u>that</u> the tenants should <u>not</u> have exits opposite the lord's corn.

But this is more likely to appear as:

Preceptum est quod . . . nullos exitus habeant—that they should have <u>no exits</u>. . . .

2. To express conditions:

(*a*) <u>If it should happen</u> that the aforesaid Simon dies without heir, let the aforesaid messuage remain to John.

Si contingat (present subjunctive, third conjugation) *quod predictus Simo obierit* (future perfect, lit., 'shall have died') *sine herede, predictum messuagium remaneat Johanni.*

(*b*) Very occasionally the following double use of the subjunctive may be met:

I give my attorney full power to act in my name just as <u>I would</u> <u>act if I were present in person</u> (NOTE the English 'were present' is rendered by imperfect subjunctive and 'would act', balancing it in thought, is also imperfect subjunctive in this type of sentence).

Do attornato meo plenam potestatem facere nomine meo sicut ego
facerem si personaliter interessem (from *intersum*)

(c) The above double subjunctive may be in the past:
He acknowledged that if his land had not been as big as the land
of his parceners, he would have taken land for himself from the
larger portion.

This requires two pluperfect subjunctives:

Recognovit quod si terra sua non fuisset (pluperfect subjunctive of
sum, Kennedy, p. 41) *tam larga quam terra parcenariorum suorum,*
terram sibi cepisset ex largiore parte.

3. To express purpose:

(a) And in order that this my gift, grant, and the confirmation of
this my present charter may stand valid and may endure inviolate forever, I have affixed my seal to this present charter.

Et ut hec mea donacio concessio et presentis carte mee confirmatio rata
stet (pres. subj. of *sto*—I stand) *et illesa imperpetuum permaneat,*
huic presenti carte sigillum meum apposui.

(b) The negative used with the subjunctive of purpose is *ne* (so
that . . . not, lest):
And they were sworn faithfully to place the boundaries between
the aforesaid men so that afterwards no (lit., not any) dispute
might be provoked between the aforesaid parties, on pain of 2s
to the lord.

Et jurati sunt fideliter metas ponere inter predictos homines ne
posterum aliqua lis mota sit (present subjunctive of *esse* with *mota*,
past participle of *moveo*, used as adjective) *inter predictas partes*
sub pena ij^s ad dominum.

4. To express a hidden question:
This is likely to occur chiefly in this type of sentence: An inquiry is
made where (when, if, whether, why, what, etc.) something is. . . .
e.g.—

Simon gives 3*d* to the lord for an inquiry to be held whether he is
the son and next heir of the same Roger.

Simo dat iii^d domino pro inquisitione habenda (to-be-held) *si sit filius*
et proximus heres ipsius Rogeri.

5. After *cum*, meaning 'although' or 'since':

e.g., *Venit Johannes de Clifton, morans in Smythforde, et conquestus est* (conqueror, deponent) *coram Rogero Gayme, tunc maiore civitatis, de hoc, quod, cum commune passagium et cariagium tam hominibus quam equis et carectis sit in vico de Flete, et a tempore quo non exstat memoria esse consuevit, quidam tamen monachus cum quibusdam servientibus abbatie, fecit fossatum in vico predicto ad impedimentum equorum et carectarum.*

(There) came J. de C., dwelling in S., and complained before R. G., then mayor of the city, of this, that, though there is a common passage and carriage way, both for men and for horses and carts in Flete Street, and it has been customary (lit., has been used to be) from time immemorial (lit., from time in which memory does not exist), nevertheless a certain monk, with certain servants of the abbey, has made a ditch in the aforesaid street, to the hindrance of horses and carts.

6. To express consequence:

e.g., Know ye that I have quitclaimed to Alice all my right . . . in all those messuages so that neither I nor my heirs nor any other in our name shall be able to exact or claim any right or claim in the aforesaid messuages from henceforth in the future, but that we may be excluded by these presents from all action of right or claim. (This use of the subjunctive from a quitclaim is so closely allied to the use expressing purpose that it hardly merits separate notice.)

Noveritis me quietumclamasse Alicie totum ius meum . . . in omnibus illis messuagiis ita quod nec ego nec heredes mei nec aliquis alius nomine nostro aliquid iuris vel clamei (lit., anything of right or claim) *in predictis messuagiis de cetero exigere vel vendicare poterimus* (future of *posse*, Kennedy, p. 62; it is derived from *esse*) *in futurum sed ab omni accione iuris et clamei simus* (that we may be, present subjunctive of *esse*) *exclusi* (past participle used simply as adjective) *per presentes.*

PRACTICE

1. *Isabella que fuit uxor Johannis finivit domino ii[s] ut possit tenere terram que fuit viri sui usque ad plenam etatem heredis predicti Johannis secundum consuetudinem manerii.*

2. *Et si contingat—quod absit*— quod dictus Henricus obierit sine herede*

* *absit:* present subjunctive of *absum.*

de corpore suo legitime exeunte (see *exiens* in Word List) *tunc tota predicta terra cum pertinenciis Alicie sorori eius integre remaneat* . . . *et si contingat quod dicta Alicia obierit sine herede de corpore suo legitime exeunte tunc tota predicta terra cum pertinenciis mihi et heredibus meis plenarie revertat.*

3. *Et ut hec nostra donatio dimissio et concessio perpetue firmitatis robur in se optineant huic carte nostre sigilla apposuimus* (or *apponi fecimus*).

4. *Loquela tangens Henricum cocum adhuc in respectum est quousque colloquium cum domino habeatur* (subjunctive of purpose).

5. *Item presentatum est quod Johannes cepit duas* (declension of *duo*; Kennedy, p. 27) *acras terre de Baldwino per scriptum viciosum; ideo preceptum est quod predictus Johannes graviter distringatur donec scriptum melius emendatur.*

6. *Redditus annuus unius rose rubre solvendus est* (is to-be-paid) *si petatur.*

7. *Et preceptum est quod illa transgressio videatur a probis et legalibus hominibus.*

8. *Preceptum est distringere Johannem et Henricum quod sint ad proximam curiam.*

9. *Item ordinatum est quod quilibet infra dominium predictum utantur pileis suis, Anglice cappes, secundum statutum.*

10. *Ballivus presentat quod Johannes Mokes habet unum lymepitt stantem infra burgum ad grave nocumentum vicinorum, ideo preceptum est quod de cetero non stetur, set omnino amoveatur, sub pena xl^s.*

1. Isabella who was the wife of John paid fine (of) 2*s* to the lord so that she could (or, might be able to) hold the land which was her husband's, until the full age of the heir of the aforesaid John, according to the custom of the manor.

2. And if it should happen—may it not be so!—(lit., may which be absent) that the said H. dies (lit., shall have died) without heir of his body lawfully issuing, then let all the aforesaid land with appurtenances remain wholly to Alice his sister . . . and if it should happen that the said A. dies without heir of her body lawfully issuing then let all the aforesaid land with appurtenances revert fully to me and my heirs.

3. And so that this our gift, demise and grant may perpetually maintain in themselves the power of stability, we have affixed our seals (or caused . . . to be fixed) to this charter.

4. The action touching Henry the cook is still in respite, until conference may be had with the lord.

5. Likewise it is presented that J. took two acres of land from Baldwin by a faulty deed; therefore it is ordered that the aforesaid J. should be severely <u>distrained</u> until the deed is better amended.

6. An annual rent of one red rose is to be paid <u>if it should be sought.</u>

7. And it is ordered that that trespass <u>should be seen</u> by honest and lawful men.

8. It is ordered to distrain J. and H. that they <u>may be</u> at the next court.

9. Likewise it is ordered that everyone soever within the aforesaid demesne <u>should wear</u> (lit., use) their caps, in English 'cappes', according to the statute.

10. The bailiff presents that J. M. has a lime-pit standing within the borough, to the grave hurt of the neighbours. Therefore it is ordered that from henceforth it be not <u>allowed-to-stand</u> (ungrammatical use of passive of this verb, with meaning indicated by context), but that <u>it be removed</u> entirely—under pain of 40s (i.e., for non-removal).

21

The gerund and gerundive: formation; uses (1)

1. Formation

(a) Gerundive: change the final *s* of the present participle to *-dus, -da, -dum.*

e.g., *habens* becomes *habendus, -a, -um* (this declines like *predictus* and agrees like an adjective).

(b) Gerund: is like the neuter form of the gerundive.

e.g., *habendum* (this declines like *pratum*; used only in singular).

NOTE. Deponents behave the same: e.g., *sequor, sequi, secutus sum*—to follow (present participle *sequens*; gerundive *sequendus, -a, -um*; gerund *sequendum*).

2. Uses (1)

Gerund

This is a verbal noun, i.e., it involves action and can be used with an object:

Nominative: none.

Accusative: *Habendum,* generally used after *ad* (*ad habendum*)—towards having, with-a-view-to having, i.e., to express purpose.

Genitive: *habendi*—of having.
Dative: *habendo*—to having, for having.
Ablative: *habendo*—by having (and sometimes after prepositions, e.g., *de, ex, in, pro*), concerning, from, in, for having.

EXAMPLES

1. *Ricardus electus est per decennarios ad levandum et colligendum redditus et perquisita curie que dominus non recepit.* R. is chosen (see Chapter 17, note (b), for tense) by the tithing-men to levy and collect (lit., towards or with a view to levying and collecting) the rents and perquisites of the court which the lord has not received.

2. *Ricardus et Robertus habent diem concordandi.* R. and R. have a day for (lit. of) coming-to-terms.

3. *Ideo data est dies Isabelle veniendo ad curiam.* So a day is given to Isabella for coming to court.

4. *... et faciendo servicia debita et consueta* ... and by doing the services owed and accustomed.

Gerundive

This is a passive verbal adjective, often implying some kind of necessity: *pecunia solvenda est*—the money is to-be-paid (note agreement with *pecunia*).

This use of the Latin gerundive is met in English in the following:

agenda—things to-be-done
memoranda—things to-be-remembered
corrigenda—things to-be-corrected
addenda—things to-be-added

(All these are neuter plural, which, when the adjective is used without a noun, gives the meaning 'things'; the singular is used similarly, e.g., *memorandum*—thing to-be-remembered.)

It is met in deeds as follows:

... dedi ... terras habendas et tenendas Johanni. ...
... I gave ... lands to-be-had and to-be-held to John. ...

(i.e., 'by' John; the dative is the rule, however, and the custom is to translate it as 'to'; deeds written in English follow this usage.)

PRACTICE

1. *Henricus invenit plegium ad solvendum domino ix^d.*
2. *Ricardus invenit plegium ad satisfaciendum domino.*
3. *Viginti solidi solvendi sunt ad quattuor anni terminos.*
4. *Sciendum est* (subject='it') *quod ego Alicia dedi terras Roberto filio meo.*
5. *Illa terra habenda et tenenda est de me eidem Philippo reddendo inde per annum decem solidos argenti.*
6. *Dedi quamdam partem terre mee in villa de Fryston, contentam infra has divisas incipiendo ad fossatum Ade Walter. ...*

1. Henry found a pledge to pay 9d to the lord.
2. Richard found a pledge to-give-satisfaction to the lord.

3. Twenty shillings are to-be-paid at the four terms of the year.

4. It is to-be-known that I, Alice, have given lands to my son Robert.

5. That land is to-be-had and to-be-held of me (lit. from me, but the custom is to translate of) to the same Philip, by rendering therefor (i.e. for it) ten shillings of silver per annum.

6. I gave a certain part of my land in the vill of Fryston, enclosed within these boundaries, beginning (lit., by beginning) at the ditch of Adam Walter. . . .

22

The gerundive: uses (2)

1. *Habendum et tendendum* in deeds.

(*a*) The properties conveyed may be various, e.g., rents, lands, tenements (*redditus*, m., *terras*, f., *tenementa*, n.; all accusative as objects of *dedi, concessi*, etc.), and properly *habenda et tenenda* (acc., n.pl.) would be used to 'agree' with these mixed genders. But the scribes often abbreviate to *habend' et tenend'* (indeed many 'endings' are abbreviated to save time, space, and trouble; the student will learn from experience how to expand the contractions and suspensions).

(*b*) The practice arises of sign-posting the successive clauses in a deed by giving the leading word a capital letter: *Sciant omnes quod ego . . . dedi . . . terras . . . Habendas et tenendas* (or *Habend' et tenend'*). This may lead to their being regarded as separate sentences, and to its being necessary to repeat the properties after *habend'*, as objects (in the accusative) of *habend'* and not of *dedi*: *Sciant omnes quod ego . . . dedi . . . terras*, etc. . . . *Habend' et tenend' predictas terras*, etc. . . . The phrase may then appear without abbreviation, and *habend' et tenend'* be regarded as an active form (rather than a passive adjective agreeing with *terras*, etc.), e.g.:

> *Habendum et tenendum predictas terras*, etc.
> There is to-be-a-having and holding the lands, etc.
> The custom is to translate simply as 'To have and to hold the aforesaid lands . . .'

2. After prepositions.

The gerundive often appears as a passive present participle, with the sense of necessity more or less submerged: *Ricardus pervenit ad plenam etatem ad terram suam habendam.* R. reached the full age for having his land (lit., for his land being-had).

BUT NOTE: *Obligor Henrico in triginta libris solvendis eidem Henrico.*

I am bound to H. in £30 to-be-paid to the same H. Here the context indicates that the idea of necessity is still in operation.

3. Improper use as active present participle.

One may sometimes meet the following ungrammatical use:

Rogerus queritur de Roberto, dicendus (or *dicendo*, by saying) *quod fabas suas asportavit.* Roger complains of Robert, saying that he carried off his beans.

PRACTICE

1. *Et portabunt aquam in prato ad falces suas acuendas.*

2. *Dedi duo messuagia Roberto . . . Habendum et tenendum predicta messuagia predicto Roberto consideratione viginti solidorum solvendorum ad duos anni terminos.*

3. *Alicia dat domino ii^d ad habendum recordum rotuli istius curie quod tenebit illam terram predictam.*

4. *Johannes dat domino iii^d pro inquisitione habenda si vero sit filius et heres predicti Gerardi.*

5. *Pro hac convencione confirmanda Simo finem fecit domino ii^s.*

6. *Preceptum est Galfrido ad ostendendam cartam ad proximam curiam.*

7. *Willelmus finivit domino xx^s ad habendam Luciam, uxorem quondam Roberti, in uxorem suam* (= as his wife), *simul cum tercia parte illius virgate ad totam vitam eorundem, faciendo omnia servicia debita et consueta.*

8. *Set ballivus respondet de l^s iii^d de firma dominicalium terrarum sic dimissarum hoc anno, tamen solebant reddere iij^li ij^s, solvendis ad duos anni terminos. Et de vi^li ij^s receptis de Johanne Naul pro firma molendini aquatici ibidem*

9. *Robertus Buckle attachiatus est ad essendum custodem vici parci, presens in curia. Et dicit quod non tenetur esse custos dicti vici, quia non est burgensis ville. Ideo quietus est.*

1. And they shall carry (in court rolls the simple future is sometimes used as an imperative) water in the meadow to sharpen their scythes (lit., with-a-view-to their scythes being-sharpened).

2. I gave two messuages to Robert. . . . To have and to hold the aforesaid messuages to the aforesaid Robert for (lit. 'by') a consideration of twenty shillings to-be-paid at the two terms of the year.

3. Alice gives 2d to the lord to have a record (lit., with-a-view-to a

record being-had) of the roll of this court that she shall hold that land aforesaid.

4. John gives 3*d* to the lord for an inquiry to-be-held (the context here indicates the translation) (as to) whether he truly is the son and heir of the aforesaid G. (The hidden question gives rise to subjunctive *sit*.)

5. For the confirmation of this agreement (lit., for this agreement being-confirmed) Simon paid 2*s* fine to the lord.

6. It is ordered to G. to show the charter at the next court. (This use after *preceptum*, *ordinatum*, etc. is very common in court rolls; the order is given with-a-view-to the charter being-shown.)

7. W. paid 20*s* fine to the lord to have Lucy (with-a-view-to Lucy being-had), wife of the late Robert, as his wife, along with the third part of that virgate for their whole life (the whole life of the same ones) by doing all services owed and accustomed.

8. But the bailiff is answerable for 50*s* 3*d* from the farm of demesne lands thus (i.e., for this sum) leased this year (though they used to yield £3. 2*s*) to-be-paid at the two terms of the year. And for £6. 2*s* received from John Naul for the farm of the water-mill there.

9. Robert Buckle is attached to be (note gerundive of *esse*,—to be) warden of Park Street; present in court. And he says that he is not bound to be warden of the said street because he is not a burgess of the town; therefore he is quit.

23

Miscellaneous items

1. (*a*) Third and fourth conjugation present indicative (active and passive): see Kennedy, pp. 46, 48, 54, 56, and use for reference.

   (*b*) All conjugations, imperfects (active and passive): see Kennedy, pp. 42, 44, 46, 48, 50, 52, 54, 56, for reference. Imperfects rarely occur in deeds, more often in court rolls; generally they are used loosely in place of the past perfect. (Properly, imperfect means 'I was doing', 'I used to do'.)

2. (*a*) Some irregular verbs: Kennedy, pp. 62–66, should be used for reference.

   NOTE that *possum* is based on *sum*.

   (*b*) Compound verbs

   Simple verbs may have their meanings modified by the addition of prepositions at their beginning:

   | *sum* (I am) | *ab* (from) | *absum*—I am away, absent |
   | | *ad* (at) | *adsum*—I am present |

   Kennedy, pp. 110–113, gives some lists of these 'compound' verbs: keep for reference.

3. Impersonal verbs

   A small number of verbs have only 'it' as subject:

   patet—it is open, plain, evident, clear
   licet—it is allowed
   placet—it pleases (with object in dative)

   These three are second conjugation and exist in all tenses.

   convenit—it is agreed; it is suitable (from the normal third-conjugation verb *convenio*, the third person singular of which may be used in this impersonal way)

   This will be most commonly found in the present or past perfect.

4. (a) Dative of possessor

Rogerus Rogero filius est—Roger is the son of Roger (lit., the son to Roger). This is not very common, but does occur.

(b) Ablative of comparison

Hic campus largior est quam ille [*campus*] (nominative after *quam*) —this field is larger than that (field).

Where *quam* is not used, the ablative of comparison appears: *Hic campus largior illo est*—this field is larger than that.

(c) Genitive of value or price: note the expression: *iiij panes, pretii j^d*—4 loaves, price 1d.

5. Pronouns

(a) *Nos, vos:* see declension, Kennedy, p. 30.
(b) Indefinite pronouns: use for reference Kennedy, pp. 89, 90, §§ 201–206.

6. *-cumque*

This added to the end of a word gives the meaning '-ever', '-soever': e.g., *qui-cumque*—whosoever, or whoever
quandocumque—whenever
ubicumque—wherever

7. *Quis,* used for 'anyone' or 'any' after *si, nisi, ne*

(a) *Ordinatum est in Gilda Aula quod omnes were, in aqua de S. posite, ammoveantur citra festum Pasche nunc proximum per ipsos qui eas in aqua predicta posuerunt; et, si quis nocumenta in aqua predicta posuerit, nisi ea tempore prenotato amoverit, solvet ad opus communitatis quadraginta solidos sterlingorum; et quod nemo deinceps talia in aqua predicta ponat sub pena predicta.*

It is ordained in the Guild-hall that all weirs, set in the water of S., should be removed (subjunctive of command) before the feast of Easter next following (lit., now next) by those who put them in the aforesaid water: and if anyone has put (lit., shall have put) harmful objects in the aforesaid water, unless he shall have removed them by the aforementioned time, he shall pay 40s sterling to the use of the community; and that no one thereafter may put (subjunctive of command) such (things) in the aforesaid water under the aforesaid penalty.

(b) *Ordinatum est de bono avisamento et pleno assensu et consensu omnium magistrorum artificii Cultellariorum huius civitatis, quod habeant* (subjunctive of command) *scrutatores inter eos annuatim eligendos, qui omnibus temporibus anni cuiuslibet quocienscumque et quandocumque eis placuerit, scrutabuntur omnes servientes predicti artificii et omnia opera sua in predicto artificio, ne* (negative purpose) *populus domini regis sit deceptus malo opere. Et ne quis* (negative command, see Chapter 20) *magister dicti artificii solvat alicui servienti suo maius stipendium pro opere suo quam vult* (from *volo*) *ordinacio artificii predicti . . .*

It is ordained by the good advice and entire assent and consent of all the masters of the craft of Cutlers of this city, that they should have searchers, to-be-chosen amongst them annually, who, at all times of any year soever, as often soever and whensoever it pleases them (lit. shall have pleased), shall examine all the servants of the aforesaid craft and all their works in the aforesaid craft, lest the Lord King's people should be cheated by bad workmanship. And that no master (lit., not any master) of the said craft should pay to any servant of his, greater wages for his work than the ordinance of the aforesaid craft lays down (lit., wills).

NOTE. The correct usage is often flouted, and *aliquis* used instead.

8. Phrases worth attention

   (a) *ex parte una . . . ex parte altera*
   on the one side (hand, part) . . . on the other
   ex parte orientali . . . ex parte occidentali
   on the east side . . . on the west side

   (b) *. . . et terra abbuttat se super terram Willelmi*
   . . . and the land abuts (lit., abuts itself) on the land of William

   (c) *. . . messuagia que quondam fuerunt dicti Thome nuper viri mei dicte Margerie*
   . . . messuages which were lately (the property) of the said Thomas, late husband <u>of me</u>, the said Margery.

   NOTE. Here *mei* is genitive of *ego*, not of *meus*, as is seen by the context.

9. Numerals

   Keep Kennedy, pp. 28, 29, for reference. Note that numeral

adverbs may be rendered: vj^{tes} for *sexies* (alternative form of *sexiens*), six times, etc.

10. Finally, a word of advice

The student will be well advised, when beginning work in his chosen field, to start with printed sources. Many of these exist (published by County Record Societies and others such as the Selden and Camden Societies), often with some English translation. In this way will be gained a confidence and facility in translation which will be of great help in surmounting the difficulties of palaeography when starting on manuscript sources, where more than half the battle consists in *knowing beforehand*, from experience, what the scribe is *likely* to have written. Two publications are indispensable guides to published records, namely, *Texts and Calendars* (by E. L. C. Mullins, London, 1958) and *Hand List of Record Publications* (by R. Somerville; British Records Association, London, 1951).

A small formulary of some common Latin documents
met with amongst local historical records:
namely gifts, bonds, powers of attorney, fines, quitclaims,
manor and borough court rolls, accounts,
and some typical ecclesiastical records

From Domesday Book

In burgo de WARWIC habet rex in dominio suo CXIII domus et barones regis habent CXII de quibus omnibus rex habet geldum suum. Episcopus de Wirecestre habet IX masuras. Episcopus de Cestre VII. Abbas de Couentreu XXXVI et IIII sunt uastae propter situm castelli . . .

Hae masurae pertinent ad terras quas ipsi barones tenent extra burgum et ibi appreciatae sunt. Praeter has supradictas masuras, sunt in ipso burgo XIX burgenses qui habent XIX masuras cum saca et soca et omnibus consuetudinibus et ita habebant tempore Regis Edwardi.

Tempore Regis Edwardi vicecomitatus de Waruuic cum burgo et cum regalibus maneriis reddebat LXV libras et XXXVI sextaria mellis aut XXIIII libras et VIII solidos pro omnibus quae ad mel pertinebant. Modo inter firmam regalium maneriorum et placita comitatus reddit per annum CXLV libras ad pondus et XXIII libras pro consuetudine canum et XX solidos pro summario et X libras pro accipitre et C solidos reginae pro gersumma. . . .

Consuetudo Waruuic fuit ut eunte rege per terram in expeditionem, decem burgenses de Waruuic pro omnibus aliis irent. Qui monitus non ibat, C solidos regi emendabat. Si vero per mare contra hostes suos ibat rex, vel IIII batsueins vel IIII libras denariorum ei mittebant.

TERRA COMITISSAE GODEVAE. In Coleshelle hundredo. COMITISSA GODEVA tenuit tempore Regis Edwardi AILSPEDE. Ibi sunt quattuor hide. Terra est VIII carrucis. Ibi sunt VIII villani et I bordarius cum II carrucis et dimidia. Silua habet I leuugam et dimidiam longitudine et unam leuugam latitudine. Tempore Regis Edwardi ualluit XL solidos et post et modo XXX solidos. Ipsa comitissa tenuit in ADERESTONE III hidas. Terra est V carrucis. Ibi sunt XI villani et II bordarii et I seruus cum IIII carrucis. Ibi VI acrae prati. Silua II leuugas longitudine et II leuugas latitudine. Valuit XL libras, modo LX solidos.

NOTE: The classical *ae* form in *uastae, hae masurae, appreciatae, praeter, quae, reginae, comitissae, Godevae, acrae.* For imperfects (*habebant*, etc.), see Chapter 23, 1 (*b*).

From Domesday Book

In the Borough of WARWICK the king has in his demesne 113 houses and the king's barons have 112, from all (of) which the king has his geld. The Bishop of Worcester has 9 messuages. The Bishop of Chester 7. The Abbot of Coventry 36, and 4 are (laid) waste for the site of the castle . . .

These messuages belong to the lands which the same barons hold outside the borough, and are valued there. Besides these above-mentioned messuages, there are in the same borough 19 burgesses who have 19 messuages with sac and soc and all customary rights and thus had (them) in the time of King Edward.

In the time of King Edward the shrievalty of Warwick with the borough and with the royal manors paid 65 pounds and 36 sesters of honey, or 24 pounds and 8 shillings for all (dues) which pertained to honey. Now, between the farm of the royal manors and the pleas of the county, it pays yearly 145 pounds by weight (*ad pondus*) and 23 pounds for the customary payment for (lit., of) dogs and 20 shillings for a sumpter-horse and 10 pounds for a hawk, and 100 shillings to the queen for a benevolence.

The custom of Warwick was that when the king went (ablative absolute: lit., the king going) by land on an expedition, ten burgesses of Warwick should go (*irent:* imperfect subjunctive after a command, 'custom' here implying an obligation) for all the others. (He) who did not go (imperfect of *eo*) when summoned, paid 100 shillings fine to the king. If however the king was going against his enemies by sea, they (i.e., the burgesses) sent him either 4 boatswains or 4 pounds of pennies.

THE LAND OF COUNTESS GODEVA. In Coleshill Hundred. Countess Godeva held Alspath in the time of King Edward. There are 4 hides. (There) is land for 8 ploughs (*carrucis:* dative meaning 'for', see Chapter 2). There are 8 villeins and 1 bordar with 2½ ploughs. The wood is (lit., has) 1½ leagues in length and 1 league in breadth. In the time of King Edward it was worth 40 shillings, and afterwards and now 30 shillings. The same countess held 3 hides in Atherstone. (There) is land for 5 ploughs. There are 11 villeins and 2 bordars and 1 serf with 4 ploughs. There are 6 acres of meadow. The wood 2 leagues in length and 2 leagues in breadth. It was worth 40 shillings, now 60 shillings.

A Gift (c. 1250)

Sciant presentes et futuri quod ego Adam filius Rogeri de Denbye dedi et concessi et hac presenti carta mea confirmavi Waltero de Floktun at heredibus suis pro homagio et servicio suo totum boscum meum in villa de Denbye sine aliquo retenemento; habendum et tenendum sibi et heredibus suis de me et heredibus meis iure hereditario libere et quiete integre plenarie cum omnibus libertatibus et esiamentis predicto bosco pertinentibus, Reddendo inde annuatim michi et heredibus meis unum denarium argenti in die Assumpcionis beate Marie Virginis pro omni seculari servicio exaccione et demanda tam forinseco domini Regis quam alio. Et ego vero et heredes mei predictum boscum Waltero predicto et heredibus suis contra omnes gentes warantizabimus et defendemus imperpetuum. Hiis testibus Johanne de Mittun, Roberto de Lintun . . . et aliis.

A Gift (1522)

Sciant presentes et futuri quod ego Willelmus Parett de Fylinghull et Elizabetha uxor mea unanimi consensu et assensu dedimus concessimus et hac presenti carta nostra confirmavimus Thome Wyghtman unum messuagium et dimidiam virgatam terre cum omnibus pertinenciis suis iacentia in villa et in campis de Fylinghull, quod quidem mesuagium quondam Willelmus Warrener rtenuit, Habendum et tenendum predictum messuagium et dimidiam virgatam tere cum omnibus suis pertinenciis in villa et in campis de Fylinghull predictis prefato Thome Wyghtman heredibus et assignatis suis libere quiete bene et in pace de capitalibus dominis feodi illius per servicia inde debita et de iure consueta, et nos vero Willelmus et Elizabetha predicti et heredes nostri predictum messuagium et dimidiam virgatam terre cum omnibus pertinenciis suis in villa et campis de Fylinghull prefato Thome Wyghtman heredibus et assignatis suis contra omnes gentes warantizabimus et imperpetuum defendemus. In cuius rei testimonium huic carte presenti nostre sigilla nostra apposuimus, Hiis testibus Willelmo Wardley, Thoma Shewall . . . et aliis. Datum apud Fylinghull xii die mensis Martii anno regni regis Henrici octavi tertio decimo.

Endorsement—Hiis testibus ad deliberacionem seisine messuagii infra specificati cum pertinenciis, videlicet Waltero Torbett de Fylinghull, gentilman, Edwardo Menny de eadem, draper, et multis aliis.

A Gift (c. 1250)

Know (men) present and future that I, Adam, son of Roger de Denbye, have given and granted and by this my present charter confirmed, to Walter de Floktun and his heirs, for his homage and service, all my wood in the vill of Denbye, without any reservation; to have and to hold to him and his heirs, of me and my heirs, by hereditary right, freely and quietly, wholly, fully, with all liberties and easements pertaining to the aforesaid wood, rendering* thence annually to me and my heirs one silver penny on the day of the Assumption of the Blessed Virgin Mary, for all secular service, exaction and demand, both foreign (service) of the lord King and other (service). And verily I and my heirs will warrant and defend against all people the aforesaid wood to the aforesaid Walter and his heirs forever. These (being) witnesses, John de Mittun, Robert de Lintun . . . and others.

A Gift (1522)

Know (men) present and future that we, Wm. Parett de Fylinghull and Elizabeth my wife with unanimous consent and assent, have given granted and by this our present charter confirmed to Thomas Wyght-man one messuage & half a virgate of land with all its appurtenances lying in the vill and in the fields of Fylinghull, which messuage indeed the late Wm. Warrener held, to have and to hold the aforesaid mes-suage and half virgate of land with all its appurtenances in the vill and fields of Fylinghull aforesaid to the aforesaid T. W., his heirs & assigns freely quietly well and in peace, of the chief lords of that fee by the services thence owed and accustomed by right, and verily we, W. & E. aforesaid, and our heirs will warrant and defend forever the aforesaid messuage and half virgate of land with all its appurtenances in the vill and fields of F. to the aforesaid T. W., his heirs and assigns, against all people. In witness of which (thing), we have affixed our seals to this our present charter, these (being) witnesses, W. Wardley, Thomas Shewall . . . and others. Given at Fylinghull on the 12th day of the month of March, in the thirteenth year of the reign of King Henry the 8th.

Endorsement—These (being) witnesses to the delivery of seisin of the messuage within-specified with appurtenances, namely W. T. de F., gentleman, E. M., of the same (place), draper, and many others.

---

* *Reddendo*—ablative of gerund—so means 'by rendering', but is generally translated simply as 'rendering'.

A Bond

Noverint universi per presentes nos Carolum Field de .... in comitatu ...., armigerum et Edwardum Field generosum filium predicti Caroli teneri et firmiter obligari Thome Stocks de .... in comitatu ......, mercer, in quinquaginta libris bone et legalis monete Anglie solvendis eidem Thome S. aut suo certo attornato vel executoribus suis ad quam quidem solutionem bene et fideliter faciendam obligamus nos et utrumque nostrum per se pro toto et in solidum heredes executores et administratores nostros firmiter per presentes sigillis nostris sigillatas Datum vicesimo nono die Augusti Anno Regni domini nostri Caroli dei gratia Anglie Scotie Francie et Hibernie Regis fidei defensoris etc. undecimo Annoque domini 1635.

Power of Attorney

Pateat per presentes quod nos Johannes de Brailes et Agnes uxor mea ordinavimus et loco nostro constituimus dilectum nobis in Christo Gilbertum de Norton attornatum nostrum ad ponendum dominum Johannem de Linley capellanum Robertum le Mercer et Willelmum le Mareschall in plena seisina in toto illo tenemento cum suis pertinenciis de quo predictos dominum Johannem Robertum et Willelmum per cartam nostram in feodum feoffavimus. Dantes eidem plenam potestatem nomine nostro facere in premissis sicut et nos faceremus si personaliter interessemus. In cuius rei testimonium hiis presentibus sigilla nostra apposuimus. Datum apud Norton die Martis proximo post festum sancti Ambrosi anno regni regis Edwardii tercii post conquestum vicesimo secundo.

A Fine

Hec est finalis concordia facta in curia domini Regis apud Westmonasterium in octava Sancti Michaelis Anno regnorum Edwardi sexti Dei gratia Anglie Francie et Hibernie regis fidei defensoris et in terra ecclesie Anglicane et Hibernice supremi capitis a conquestu quinto coram Henrico Makin, Ricardo Hunte et Edwardo Leke Justiciariis et aliis domini regis fidelibus tunc ibi presentibus INTER Willelmum Stone armigerum et Nicholaum Stone generosum querentes et Johannem Barton et Agnetem Colford viduam sororem

A Bond

Know all men by (these) presents that we, Charles Field of........ in the county of ...., esquire, and Edward Field, gentleman, son of the aforesaid Charles, are held and firmly bound (lit., know us to be held & to be firmly bound) to Thomas Stocks of .... in the county of ...., mercer, in fifty pounds of good and lawful money of England to be paid to the same Thomas S. or his certain attorney or his executors, to making which payment indeed well and faithfully, we bind ourselves and each of us by himself for the whole (sum), and (we bind) for the whole our heirs executors and administrators firmly by these presents sealed with our seals. Given on the 29th August in the eleventh year of the reign of our lord Charles by the grace of God King of England Scotland France and Ireland defender of the faith, etc., and in the year of the Lord 1635.

Power of Attorney

Be it known by (these) presents that we, John de Brailes & Agnes my wife have appointed and set up in our place Gilbert de Norton, beloved to us in Christ, (as) our attorney for placing Master John de Linley, chaplain, Robert le Mercer & William le Mareschall in full seisin in all that tenement with its appurtenances, of which, by our charter, we have enfeoffed in fee the aforesaid Master John, Robert and William. Giving to the same full power in our name to act in the premises just as we would act if we were present in person. In witness of which we have affixed our seals to these presents. Given at Norton on Tuesday next after the feast of St. Ambrose in the 22nd year of the reign of King Edward the Third after the conquest.

A Fine

This is the final agreement made in the court of the lord King at Westminster in the octave of St. Michael in the fifth year of the reigns of Edward the Sixth from the conquest, by grace of God King of England, France and Ireland, defender of the faith and supreme head on earth of the church of England and Ireland, before the Justices Henry Makin, Richard Hunte, and Edward Leke, and other faithful (subjects) of the lord king then there present, BETWEEN Wm. Stone esquire, and Nicholas Stone, gentleman, querents, and John Barton

dicti Johannis deforciantes de uno mesuagio in Colford situato cum omnibus suis pertinenciis unde placitum convencionis summonitum fuit inter eos in eadem curia VIDELICET quod predicti J. B. et Agnes recognoverunt predictum messuagium cum pertinenciis esse ius ipius Willelmi Stone ut illud quod iidem W. et N. Stone habuerunt de dono predictorum J. B. et Agnetis et illud remiserunt et quietum clamaverunt de ipsis Johanne B. et Agnete et heredibus ipius Johannes predictis Willelmo Stone et Nicholao et heredibus ipius Willelmi imperpetuum ET PRETEREA iidem J. B. et Agnes concesserunt pro se et heredibus ipius Johannis quod ipsi warantizabunt predicto W. Stone et Nicholao et heredibus ipius Willelmi predictum messuagium cum pertinenciis contra omnes homines imperpetuum et pro hac recognicione remissione quieta clamatione warantia fine et concordia iidem W. Stone et Nicholaus Stone dederunt predictis Johanni B. et Agneti quadraginta libras sterlingorum.

Quitclaim (1427)

Noverint universi per presentes me Robertum Hall, de Rigton, parker, remisisse relaxasse et omnino pro me et heredibus meis imperpetuum quietumclamasse Willielmo Forde, de Hawley pewtrer, heredibus et assignatis suis totum ius meum et clameum que habui habeo seu quovismodo in futurum habere potero in duobus croftis cum suis pertinenciis in Rigton et dicta crofta iacent inter terram quam Johannes Lyghtfot quondam tenuit ex parte una et terram vocatam le holowfelde ex parte altera in latitudine et extendunt se in longitudine de Grenesplace usque ad terram vocatam Nomanneslonde ac venellam ducentem usque Hawley Churche sicut se plenarie proportant per metas et divisas ibidem factas Ita quod nec ego predictus Robertus nec heredes mei nec aliquis alius nomine meo seu nomine nostro aliquid ius vel clameum in croftis predictis cum singulis suis pertinenciis de cetero exigere seu vendicare poterimus set per presentes ab omni accione iuris imperpetuum simus exclusi presentes sigillo meo signavi Datum apud Hawley die Martis proximo post festum sancti Michaelis Archangeli anno regni Regis Henrici sexti post conquestum sexto.

and Agnes Colford, widow, sister of the said John, deforciants, concerning one messuage situated in Colford, with all its appurtenances,
concerning which a plea of covenant had been summoned between
them in the same court . . . NAMELY that the aforesaid J. B. and
Agnes have recognized the aforesaid messuage with appurtenances to
be the right of the same* Wm. Stone, as (being) that which the same
W. and N. Stone had of the gift of the aforesaid J. B. and A. and they
(i.e., J. B. & A.) remise it and quitclaim for the same J. B. and Agnes
and the heirs of John himself, to the aforesaid Wm. S. and N., and the
heirs of Wm. himself forever, AND MOREOVER the same J. B. and
A. have granted for themselves and the heirs of the same J. that they
themselves will warrant to the aforesaid W. S. and N. and to the heirs
of the same Wm., the aforesaid messuage with appurtenances against
all men forever, and for this acknowledgement, remise, quitclaim,
warrant, fine and agreement, the same W. S. and N. S. have given to
the aforesaid J. B. and Agnes forty pounds of sterling.

Quitclaim (1427)

Know all men by (these) presents that I, Robert Hall of Rigton, parker,
have remised, released and entirely quitclaimed forever for myself and
my heirs to Wm. Forde of Hawley, pewterer, and his heirs and assigns
all my right and claim which I had, have, or in any way henceforth
could have, in two crofts with their appurtenances in Rigton, and the
said crofts lie between the land which John Lyghtfot lately held, on
the one hand, and the land called the Holowfelde on the other, in
width, and in length they extend from Grenesplace to the land called
Nomanneslonde and a lane leading to Hawley Church, as they fully
appear by the bounds and divisions there made. So that (i.e., in order
that) neither I the aforesaid Robert nor my heirs nor any other in my
name or in our name may be able henceforth to demand any right or
lay (any) claim in the aforesaid crofts with all their appurtenances,
but by (these) presents we may be excluded forever from all legal
action, I have stamped these presents with my seal. Given at Hawley
on Tuesday next after the feast of St. Michael the Archangel, in the
6th year of the reign of King Henry the Sixth after the conquest.

---

* *ipius:* so common a contraction for *ipsius* that it is often written thus without
any mark of contraction—translated as 'the same' to help the English.

Probate Copy of a Will

In Dei nomine Amen. In vigilia Sancti Jacobi Apostoli A.D. millesimo cccc^{mo}, ego Nicholaus Westerne, ville de S., grocer, compos mentis licet eger in corpore, condo testamentum meum in hunc modum. In primis lego animam meam Deo omnipotenti, beate Marie virgini et omnibus sanctis eius, corpusque meum ad sepeliendum in ecclesia parochiali Sancti Michaelis de S., iuxta Sarram Westerne, nuper uxorem meam. Item lego et volo quod omnia debita mea de bonis meis plenarie persolvantur. Item lego domino Gilberto Bradley rectori ecclesie pariochalis predicte iij^s iiij^d. Item lego fabrice ecclesie pariochialis predicte iij^s iiij^d .... Item lego Agneti filie mee et heredibus eius de proprio corpore legitime procreatis unum burgagium cum suis pertinenciis situatum in villa de S. in quodam vico vocato Welle Strete in quo modo habito, inter tenementum Rogeri Baker et tenementum Johannis Warde Habendum et tenendum etc..................

.... Et si contingat quod dicta Agnes obierit absque heredibus tunc lego et do predictum burgagium custodibus, quicumque sint, ecclesie pariochalis predicte de S. Item lego omnia residua bonorum meorum non legatorum debitis meis prius solutis filie mee predicte. Huius autem testamenti mei executorem meum ordino facio et constituo dilectum mihi in Christo Willelmum White.

Dorse) Probatum fuit presens testamentum coram nobis officiali domini Archiadiaconi D. in ecclesia pariochali de S. die Sabbati............... unde commissa exstitit* infrascripto executore administratio bonorum dicti defuncti in forma iuris.

---

* See Word List for *existo*.

Probate Copy of a Will

In the name of God, Amen. On the eve of St. James Apostle, 1400 A.D., I, Nicholas Westerne, of the town of S., grocer, (being) of sound mind (lit. sound of mind) though sick in body, make my will in this wise. Firstly I leave my soul to God Almighty, to the Blessed Virgin Mary and all His saints, and my body to-be-buried in the parish church of St. Michael of S., by the side of Sarah Westerne, my late wife. Item I leave and will that all my debts be fully discharged (pres. subj.*) from my goods. Item I leave to Master Gilbert Bradley rector of the aforesaid parish church, 3s 4d. Item I leave to the fabric of the aforesaid parish church 3s 4d...................................... Item I leave to Agnes, my daughter, and her heirs of her own body lawfully begotten, one burgage with its appurtenances situated in the town of S., in a certain street called Welle Street, in which I now dwell, between the tenement of Roger Baker and the tenement of John Warde. To have and to hold etc...............................
.... And if it should happen that the said Agnes should die without heirs then I leave and give the aforesaid burgage to the wardens, whosoever they may be (pres. subj.†), of the aforesaid parish church of S. Item I leave all the rest of my goods not bequeathed after the payment of my debts (lit. my debts having first been paid—ablative absolute), to my daughter aforesaid. But of this my will I appoint, make and set up as my executor, my beloved in Christ, William White.
(Dorse) The present will was proved before us, Official of Master Archdeacon D., in the parish church of S. on Saturday.............. where administration of the goods of the said deceased was committed to the executor overleaf (lit., within-written) in legal form.

---

* After the command.
† The subjunctive here indicates possibility rather than fact. *Quicumque sunt* would mean 'whosoever they are'.

Some Typical Manor Court Proceedings

Halton

Curia prima domini Roberti de Halton tenta ibidem cum visu franciplegii in crastino Sancte Lucie virginis anno regni regis Ricardi secundi post conquestum xviij⁰

Essonia

Johannes Broun de communi per Willelmum Brid Plegiu Robertus North primo

Johannes Middlemor	*Rogerus Smalbroke*
Ricardus de Fulford	*Adam le Walker*
Willelmus Sidenhale	*Thomas atte Birch*
Henricus Gerard	*Simon de Otleye*
Iohannes Wodard	*Willelmus Wodekok*

fidelitas

Omnes isti fecerunt domino fidelitatem et cognoverunt tenere de domino ut inferius

Redditus
assisus ix^d

opera relaxata
ij^s

customarius

Johannes Wodard venit ad istam curiam et cognovit tenere de domino unum tenementum et x acras terre Reddendo inde per annum de redditu assiso ix^d Et pro operibus in parte sibi relaxatis per annum ij^s Et ulterius cognovit quod debet falcare et elevare unam acram prati et iij rodas Et habebit primo die jentaculum Et debet metere in autumpno cum uno homine per viii dies Et erit in mensa domini in prandio et cena Et debet reddere sarculare bladum domini cum j homine per unum diem sine cibo . . . . Et debet sectam curie de tribus in tres Et servare dictum tenementum sine vasto et distruxione Et habet diem ad ostendendum qualiter intravit. . . . .

. . . . .

Redditus iiij^d

Presentatum est per omnes tenentes quod Robertus Birche tenet j cotagium cum curtilagio reddendo inde per annum pro omnibus iiij^d

Firma xiij^s iiij^d

Dies

Item presentatum est quod Ricardus Wallere tenet de domino ad firmam xxx acras per estimacionem communem Et reddit inde per annum xiij^s iiij^d Et habet diem ad ostendendum qualiter tenet &c citra proximam curiam

Some Typical Manor Court Proceedings

Halton	The first court of the lord Robert of Halton, held there with view of frankpledge, in the morrow of St. Lucy, Virgin, in the 18th year of the reign of King Richard the Second after the Conquest
Essoin	John Broun (essoined) of common (suit) by William Brid. Pledge Robert North. The first (time)
Fealty	John Middlemor etc. Roger Smalbroke etc
	All these have done* fealty to the lord and acknowledged that they (*se* understood) hold of the lord as below
Fixed rent 9d	John Wodard has come to this court and acknowledged that he holds of the lord one tenement and ten acres of land, rendering in respect thereof 9d per annum (of)
day-works remitted 2s	fixed rent, and for day-works in part remitted to him, 2s per annum. And further he has acknowledged that he is obliged to mow and lift one acre and three roods of meadow. And he shall have breakfast on the first day.
customary tenant	And he is obliged to reap in the autumn with one man for eight days. And he shall be at the lord's table at dinner and supper. And he is obliged to render weeding (lit., to weed) the lord's corn with one man for one day without food ....
	And he owes suit of court every three weeks (lit., from three (weeks) to three (weeks)) And to keep the said tenement without damage or waste. And he has a day to show by what right he has entered (i.e., the tenement) ....
Rent 4d	It is presented by all the tenants that Robert Birche holds one cottage with curtilage, rendering in respect thereof 4d per annum for all (dues)
	Likewise it is presented that Richard Wallere holds of the lord at farm (i.e., at fixed payment) thirty acres
Farm 13s 4d	according to the common reckoning. And he pays in
Day	respect thereof 13s 4d per annum. And he has a day to show by what right he holds etc. . . . before the next court

* The past perfect verbs have been translated as 'have done', etc., rather than 'did', etc., as this is more in keeping with the sense of proceedings being recorded on the spot.

Districtio Preceptum est distringere Sibillam Freberne pro fidelitate domino facienda . . . .

Visus Franciplegii tentus ibidem die et anno ut supra

Districtio Johannes Heydon decennarius cum sua decenna presentat quod Willelmus Happesforde mansit infra dominium domini per j annum et amplius et non est in decenna Ideo preceptum est eum distringere citra proximam curiam ad ponendum &c

Tastator
Misericordie
vi^a Rogerus Lalleforde tastator ibidem presentat quod Sarra Tubbinge ij (iiij^d) et Johannes Corwen j (ij^d) braciaverunt et fregerunt assisam ideo remanent in misericordia

Pena Ricardus Merton decennarius ibidem cum sua decenna presentat quod via regia apud Merton est submersa ad commune nocumentum defectu scuracionis fossati Willelmi White ideo remanet in misericordia Et preceptum est scurare dictum fossatum citra proximam curiam sub pena xl^d

Summa huius Visus vj^d

Afferatores Johannes Middlemor
Ricardus de Fulford

Some Typical Borough Court Proceedings

Freshville Curia burgi tenta ibidem die Lune . . . .

Misericordie
vj^a Prepositi burgi presentant quod Johannes Gerard (ij^d) Ricardus Bakere (ij^d) et Johanna Bakeres (ij^d) pistores fecerunt panem album minus ponderis prout coram eis compertum est hac vice prima Et quod filius Henrici Davy carnifex vendit carnes suas extra communes stallas ubi ex antiquo ordinatum fuit contra defensum Ideo ipse in misericordia

Distraint — An order is made (lit., it is ordered) to distrain Sibil Freberne to do fealty to the lord (lit., for fealty to-be-done)

View of Frankpledge held at the same place on the day and year as above

Distraint — John Heydon, tithing-man, with his tithing, presents that William Happesforde has dwelt within the lord's demesne for one year and more, and is not in a tithing. Therefore an order is made to distrain him before the next court to be placed (i.e., in a tithing), etc.

Ale-taster — Roger Lalleforde ale-taster at the same place presents that Sarah Tubbinge twice (4d) and John Corwen once

Amercements 6d — (2d) have brewed and broken the assize; therefore they remain in mercy

Richard Merton, tithing-man at the same place, with his tithing, presents that the king's highway at Merton is flooded to the common hurt, from lack of scouring of William White's ditch; therefore he remains in mercy. And an order is made to scour the said ditch before the

Penalty — next court—under pain of 40d (i.e. for noncompliance with order)

> Total of this View   6d
>
> Affeerers   John Middlemor
> Richard de Fulford

Some Typical Borough Court Proceedings

Freshville — Court of the Borough held there on Monday......

The reeves of the borough present that John Gerard (2d) Richard Bakere (2d) and Joan Bakeress (2d), bakers, have made white bread below weight (lit., less of weight) as was found before them (i.e., in another court). This

Amercements 6d — the first time (i.e., first offence). And that the son of Henry Davy, butcher, sold his meat(s) outside the common stalls where of old it has been the regulation (lit., been ordained) (i.e., to sell it)—contrary to the prohibition. Therefore he is in mercy.

Misericordia *iij^a*	*Et quod Johannes Grey (iij^a) non facit iiij^{or} panes pro denario prout de iure debet secundum statutum et proclamationem ad nocumentum patrie Ideo ipse in misericordia*
Districtio	*Adhuc distringere Ricardum Lovot ad respondendum Johanni Birch in placito debiti*
Misericordia *ij^a* *Districtio*	*Thomas Freeman in misericordia (ij^a) quia non habet Willelmum Box ad respondendum dominis quare obstruxit et artavit fossatum ville ad nocumentum commune ideo preceptum est distringere dictum Willelmum contra proximam curiam*
Attachiare	*Robertus Box attachiatus est per j caudron, precii iij^a, ad respondendum Johanni Wain in placito convencionis, et non se justificat Ideo preceptum est hoc retinere et melius attachiare contra proximam curiam*
Pipoudre *xij^a*	*Pypoudre xij^a*
Misericordia *vj^a*	*Rogerus Scmale in misericordia quia Felicia Liberd iuste levavit hutesium super ipsum Plegius Johannes Birch*
Misericordia *iij^a*	*Sibilla Cole in misericordia quia communis garilatrix et pacis perturbatrix*
Misericordia *xij^a*	*Eadem Sibilla (vj^a) Hugo Saly (vj^a) in misericordia quia sunt communes regratores piscium*
Misericordia *ij^a*	*Joh. Webbe in misericordia pro licencia concordandi cum Ricardo Perks in placito transgressionis*

. . . .

Electio	*Prepositi burgi* *Walterus Michel et Ricardus Freberne* *Ballivi* *Willelmus Happesforde et Thomas Page* *Custodes*—*extra* portam orientalem *Nicholaus Broun* et *Johannes Birch* —*infra* port. orient. *Johannes Hopkyns* et *Willelmus Forde*

. . . .

	De perquisitis curie	. . . .
Summa	*De pypoudre*	. . . .
	In expensis senescalli et aliorum	. . . .
	Et in pargamino	. . . .

80

Amercement 3d	And that John Grey (3d), to the district's hurt, does not make 4 loaves for a penny, as lawfully he should, according to the statute and proclamation. Therefore he is in mercy.
Distraint	Still to distrain Richard Lovot to answer to John Birch in a plea of debt
Amercement 2d	Thomas Freeman in mercy (2d), because he has not Wm. Box to answer to the lords why he has obstructed and choked the town ditch to the common hurt.
Distraint	Therefore an order is made to distrain the said William against (i.e., before) the next court.
To attach	Robert Box is attached by one cauldron, value 3d, to answer to John Wain in a plea of covenant, and he does not justify himself. Therefore an order is made to to keep it (i.e., the cauldron) and to attach more heavily (lit., better) before the next court
Piepowder 12d	Piepowder 12d
Amercement 6d	Roger Scmale in mercy because Felicia Liberd rightly raised the hue & cry on him. Pledge—John Birch
Amercement 3d	Sybil Cole in mercy, because she (is) a common scold and disturber of the peace
Amercement 12d	The same Sybil (6d), & Hugh Saly (6d), in mercy, because they are common regraters of fish
Amercement 2d	John Webb in mercy for licence to agree (lit., of agreeing) with Richard Perks in a plea of trespass

. . . .

Election	Reeves of the borough—Walter Michel & Richard Freberne
	Bailiffs—Wm. Happesforde & Thomas Page
	Wardens—
	outside the East Gate—Nicholas Broun & John Birch
	within the East Gate—John Hopkyns & Wm. Forde

. . . .

	Of profits of the Court	. . . .
Total	Of Piepowder	. . . .
	In expenses of Steward and others	. . . .
	And in parchment	. . . .

Accounts

The following are extracts from accounts. No attempt has been made to balance the figures.

Bailiff's Account

Compotus Roberti Clerk, ballivi .... *per unum annum integrum*

Arreragia

Nulla habet quia idem computans in ultimo compoto suo inde recessit in excessu

Summa nulla

Redditus Assisi

Set respondet de v^s iiij^d de redditu assiso diversorum tenentium domini in quodam vico infra villam, vocato Smythestrete, solvendis ad quattuor anni terminos principales equaliter, sicut continetur in compoto precedente

Summa v^s iiij^d

Firma Pasture

Et de x^{li} de firma pasture cuiusdam pasture vocate le Feld sic dimisse Thome Blake hoc anno, tamen solebat reddere xvj^{li} per annum, ut dicit super sacramentum suum

Summa x^{li}

Vendicio Bosci

De proficuo proveniente de venditione bosci sive subbosci ibidem videlicet per tempus predictum non respondet, eo quod responsum est domino de proficuis provenientibus de vendicione bosci sive subbosci predictorum per Thomam Liber subforestarium ibidem, sicut continetur in compoto suo de dicto officio suo per tempus supradictum reddito

Summa nulla

Summa Totalis Receptionum.......

Decasus Redditus

Et in decasu redditus unius tenementi in Smythforde nuper in tenura Willelmi Fox pro xvij^s per annum et sic superius onerati hoc anno, eo quod modo dimittitur solomodo pro xiij^s iiij^d per annum—iij^s viij^d

Et in allocacione redditus unius tenementi in vico alto nuper Rogeri Broun, in tenura Johannis Byrde, eo quod erronice et iniuste superius oneratur ad vj^d per annum sicut continetur in dicto rentali—vj^d

Summa iiij^s ij^d

Bailiff's Account

The account of Robert Clerk, bailiff . . . . for one whole year

Arrears

He has none because the same accountant at his last account withdrew therefrom with a surplus

Total Nil

Fixed Rents (i.e., Rents of Assize)

But he is answerable for 5s 4d from the fixed rent of divers tenants of the lord in a certain street within the vill called Smythstrete, to-be-paid at the four chief terms of the year, in equal parts, as is contained in the preceding account

Total 5s 4d

Farm of Pasture

And for £10 from farm of pasture of a certain pasture called the Feld thus (i.e., for this sum) leased to Thomas Blake this year, though it used to yield £16 per annum, as he says upon his oath

Total £10

Sale of Wood

For profit issuing from sale of wood or coppice-wood there, that is for the aforesaid period, he is not answerable, because a return has been made (lit., it has been answered) to the lord of profits issuing from sale of wood or coppice-wood aforesaid, by Thomas Liber, under-forester there, as is contained in his account of his said office rendered for the aforesaid time

Total Nil
Sum Total of Receipts. . . . .

Decay of Rent

And in decay of rent of one tenement in Smythforde [lately in the tenure of William Fox for 17s per annum and thus (i.e., for this sum) above charged for this year] because it is now leased at only 13s 4d per annum—3s 8d

And in allowance of rent of one tenement in the High Street, lately Roger Broun's, in the tenure of John Byrde, because it is wrongly and unjustly above charged at 6d per annum, as is contained in the said rental—6d

Total 4s 2d

Reparaciones

Et in diversis misis, custubus, et expensis per ipsum computantem factis et appositis super necessaria pro reparacione tenementorum ibidem hoc anno, ut patet particulariter per unam billam inde super hunc compotum liberatam et inter memoranda eiusdem remanentem xxj^{li} x^s j^d ob.

Summa xxj^{li} x^s j^d ob.

Expense Senescalli

Et in expensis senescalli tenentis curias ibidem hoc anno, ut patet per unam billam inde restitutam ac inter memoranda predicta remanentem ultra xj^s pro expensis dicti senescalli allocatos in compoto ballivi burgi ibidem—xxv^s
Et in expensis ipsius computantis equitantis ad Lincolniam pro diversis negotiis supradictis terris et tenementis ibidem pertinentibus ut patet per unam billam inde restitutam—vj^s j^d

Summa xxxj^s j^d

Liberacio denariorum

Et in denariis per eundem computantem receptori domini liberatis super hunc compotum coram auditore—lv^s vj^d

Summa lv^s vj^d
Summa totalis allocacionum . . . .

Et predictus ballivus seu computans ab isto compoto recessit quietus

---

Churchwardens' Account

Compotus Ade Ledbetere et Willelmi Manne custodum beate Marie Ecclesie pariochalis . . . .

Arreragia

Iidem respondent de ij^{li} v^s ij^d as quadrante de arreragiis compoti anni precedentis

Summa   ij^{li} v^s ij^d quadrans

Redditus

Et de cv^s ij^d de certo redditu assise ibidem
Et de xij^d de incremento redditus j cotagii extra portam occidentalem

Summa   cvj^s ij^d

Repairs

And in divers outlays, costs and expenses made by the accountant himself and applied to necessaries for the repair of tenements there this year, as appears in detail in a bill in respect thereof, handed over at this audit, and remaining amongst its memoranda £21 10s 1½d

Total £21 10s 1½d

Steward's Expenses

And in the expenses of the steward (in) holding courts there this year, as appears in a bill returned in respect thereof and remaining amongst the aforesaid memoranda (over & above 11s allowed for expenses of the said steward in the account of the bailiff of the borough there)—25s
And in the expenses of the accountant himself (in) riding to Lincoln on divers affairs pertaining to the aforesaid lands & tenements there (i.e., in the manor of which he is bailiff), as appears in a bill returned in respect thereof—6s 1d

Total 31s 1d

Payment of Moneys

And in moneys paid by the same accountant to the lord's receiver at this audit, in the presence of the auditor—55s 6d

Total 55s 6d

Sum Total of allowances ....

And the aforesaid bailiff or accountant withdraws quit from this audit

---

Churchwardens' Account

The Account of Adam Ledbetere & William Manne, wardens of the parish church of St. Mary ....

Arrears

The same (wardens) are answerable for £2 5s 2¼d arrears of the account of the preceding year

Total £2 5s 2¼d

Rent

And for 105s 2d from a certain rent of assize there
And for 12d from an increase of rent of one cottage outside the West gate

Total 106s 2d

Receptiones Forinsece

Et de ij^s receptis de candelis venditis pro sepulturis diversis

Summa ij^s

Summa totalis receptionum ....

Expense

In xv libris cere emptis ix^s iiij^d ob. (pretium libre vij^d ob.)
In expensis dictorum custodum euntium pro negotio beate Marie expediendo apud Longdon per ij dies ij^s j^d obolus
In emendando domum ubi capellanus beate Marie moratur ij^s

Summa omnium expensarum et liberationum ....
Et sic debent de claro...

Account re Work on Parish Church

Compotus Willelmi le Walker receptoris nomine operis in ecclesia pariochali........ *per unum annum integrum*

Denarii de Burgo

Idem respondet de x^{li} x^s ij^d receptis de Johanne White custode per talliam

Denarii de executoribus testamentorum

Et de iij^s receptis de Ricardo Fox executore testamenti Thome Wyn Et de xv^s receptis de Thoma Blake executore testamenti Felicie uxoris sue

Denarii ex devocione

Et de xx^s receptis de Johanne Greene ex devocione

Summa totalis receptorum supra ....

De Quibus

Solvit Johanni Wode fodiatori petrarum, per vices, xxj^s ij^d
Solvit Rogero Widdop pro diversis facturis, per vices, una cum ferro suo proprio et stipendio, xxv^s vj^d

Summa ....

Liberatum Johanni Bagot per indenturam una vice iiij^{l}j

Summa omnium expensarum et liberationum ....

Et debet ....

Postea allocatum eidem ....

86

Outside Receipts

And for 2s received from sale of candles (lit., candles sold) for divers burials

Total 2s

Sum Total of Receipts . . . .

Paid Out

On 15 lbs wax purchased 9s 4½d (price of 1 lb—7½d)

On expenses of said wardens travelling to expedite business of St. Mary's at Longdon—for two days—2s 1½d

On repairing the house where dwells the chaplain of St. Mary's—2s

Total of all expenses and payments. . . . .

And thus they owe. . . . . net

Account re Work on Parish Church

The Account of Wm. le Walker, receiver in respect of (lit., in the name of) the work on the parish church, ... for one whole year

Moneys from the Borough

The same (receiver) is answerable for £10 10s 2d received by tally from John White, warden

Moneys from the executors of wills

And for 3s received from Richard Fox executor of the will of Thomas Wyn And for 15s received from Thomas Blake executor of the will of Felicia his wife

Moneys from donation

And for 20s received from John Green as (lit., from) donation

Sum Total of receipts above . . . .

Whereof (lit., from which)

He has paid to John Wode, quarryman (lit., digger of stones), at various times, 21s 2d

He has paid to Roger Widdop, for various works, at various times, together with his own iron and stipend, 25s 6d

Total . . . .

Paid to John Bagot by an indenture, on one occasion £4

Total of all expenses and payments   . . . .

And he owes   . . . .

Afterwards allowed to the same (receiver)   . . . .

Some Items from a Chapter Act Book

Anno Incarnacionis Christi Millesimo cccc liiij^{to}
Capitulum celebratum ij° die Novembris anno prenotato
Alicia Ellys dicitur esse ribalda et defamatrix suorum vicinorum. Citata comparuit et negat articulum, et habet diem ad proximum (capitulum), quo die defecit in purgacione. Ideo fustigata vj^{ies} circa ecclesiam diebus dominicis

Ricardus Clere de Westgate, taillour, et Johanna uxor Johannis Nichol de Northgate, baker, admissi sunt ministratores bonorum Agnetis Wylson, nuper de Bedernbank, ab intestato discedentis. Ej jurati sunt ad inventarium et compotum exhibenda, et inde habent commissionem, et composuerunt cum officio pro ij^s

Thomas Grange citatus ad instanciam Ricardi Burnet in causa lesionis fidei prestite pro v^s solvendis in festo Ascensionis Domini ultimo elapso, comparuit et fatetur articulos et habuit diem solvendi in festo Omnium Sanctorum ex tunc proximo sequente et super hoc prestitit juramentum et solvit iiij^d nomine expensarum

....

Henricus Pyper peciit Agnetem Cotte citari in causa lesionis fidei et extunc condempnari ij^s in quibus tenetur. Comparuit per procuratorem qui procurator ministrato ei articulo negat se fidem dedisse unde dies Sabati proxime sequens est ei assignata ad publice producendos testes super probacionem fidei.

Satisfecit termino producendo duos testes, scilicet Robertum Benne, qui juratus deposuit quod ivit* cum Johanne Broun ad domum Agnetis Cotte, et ibidem audivit ipsum Johannem supradictum interpellantem sepedictam Agnetem pro quadam summa pecunie, videlicet ij^s, ut credit, que dixit quod solveret† predictam summam in duobus festis, scilicet in festo Purificationis beate Marie, et ad festum Visitationis beate Marie solveret† reliquam partem summe. Interrogatus utrum ad hoc perimplendum prestiterit fidem, dixit quod sic, ut putat, quod videbat manus ipsorum junctas.

---

* See *eo* in Word List.

† *solveret*: imperfect subjunctives to express 'would pay'. This is the usual practice in medieval Latin in a phrase of this kind, after words like 'said', 'denied', etc.

Some Items from a Chapter Act Book

In the one thousand four hundred and fifty-fourth year of the Incarnation of Christ

Chapter held 2nd day of November in the year before mentioned

Alice Ellys is said to be foul-tongued and a slanderer of her neighbours. Being cited,* she appeared and denies the article, and has a day till the next (chapter), on which day she failed in compurgation. Therefore whipped round the church six times on Sundays.

Richard Clere of Westgate, tailor, and Joan, wife of John Nicol of Northgate, baker, were admitted (as) administrators of the goods of Agnes Wylson, late of Bedernbank, (she) dying intestate. And they were sworn to exhibit the inventory and account (*exhibenda*, n.pl., to agree with the two mixed genders—*inventarium*, n., *compotus*, m.), and then they are commissioned (lit., have the commission), and they compounded with the office for 2s.

Thomas Grange being cited* at the instance of Richard Burnet, in a case of breach of faith pledged for 5s to be paid at the feast of the (Lord's) Ascension last past, appeared, and confesses the articles, and had a day for paying (lit., of paying) at the feast of All Saints thereafter next following, and he took his oath on this, and paid 4d costs (lit., in respect of expenses)

Henry Pyper petitioned (*peciit*, i.e., *petiit*, short for *petivit*) that Agnes Cotte be cited (lit., A. C. to be cited—pres. inf. pass.) in a case of breach of faith, and thereupon be mulcted 2s in which she is bound. She appeared by proctor, which proctor, the article being administered to him (abl. absolute), denies that he (identifying himself with Agnes) gave a pledge, whereupon Saturday next following is assigned to him (i.e., Henry) to produce publicly witnesses in proof of the pledge.

He complied with (lit., satisfied) the time-limit by producing two witnesses, namely Robert Benne, who being sworn,* deposed that he went with John Broun to the house of A. C., and there heard the same John aforesaid calling upon the oft-mentioned Agnes for a certain sum of money, viz. 2s, as he believes, who (i.e., Agnes) said that she would pay (imperf. subj.) the aforesaid sum on two feasts, namely on the feast of the Purification (of Blessed Mary), and at the feast of the Visitation (of Blessed Mary) she would pay the remaining part of the sum. Being asked* whether she pledged her troth (*prestiterit*—perf. subj.—because of the 'hidden question') to fulfill this (promise), he said yes, he thought so, because he saw their hands joined.

* Past participles, lit., 'having been cited', etc.

Et alter testis Johannes Broun juratus deposuit quod transitum penes domum dicte Agnetis fecit et secum accepit Robertum Benne, ut ipse audiret communicacionem inter eos habitam, unde ipse eam in domum inveniens, peciit ab ea summam ij^s quos debuit Henrico Pyper. Ipsa prebuit responsum quod solveret* eandem summam in festis, scilicet Purificacionis beate Marie et relictam partem summe in festo Visitationis beate Marie.

Pars adversa peciit diem ad obiciendum contra dicta testium. Habuit diem Mercurii proxime sequentem in quo nec comparuit personaliter nec per procuratorem, unde propter eius contumaciam erat suspensa, et dies Mercurii assignata est proxime sequens festum Sancti Thome partibus ad audiendam sententiam diffinitivam.

Partibus presentibus sententia lata† erat sub hac forma: Ut Agnes Cotte solveret‡ ij^s iiij^d scilicet in 2^{bus} festis; prima solucio esset‡ in festo Assumpcionis beate Marie, scilicet xx^d, secunda solucio in festo Michaelis, scilicet xx^d, ad quam quidem solucionem faciendam fideliter corporale prestitit iuramentum.

NOTE. The following ecclesiastical extracts present considerably more difficulty than anything dealt with so far. The Latin is closer than usual to classical Latin, and the order of words and phrases correspondingly further from English usage. As in the rest of the book, translations have been kept fairly literal to help the student to understand how they are arrived at.

An Institution and Induction from a Chapter Act Book

Universis Christi fidelibus pateat per presentes quod nos capitulum ecclesie collegiate de W., ... diocesis, dominum Johannem Piers presbiterum dicte diocesis ad vicariam canonicatus et prebende de Wessle in ecclesia dicta de W., per mortem domini Thome Lambe, capellani, ultimi vicarii ejusdem, vacantem, et ad presentacionem Magistri Willelmi Manne, canonici dicte ecclesie et prebendarii prebende predicte de Wessle in eadem, vere ejusdem vicarie patroni, canonice admisimus, ac ipsum dominum Johannem Piers perpetuum vicarium in forma ordinacionis super admissionem vicariorum dicte ecclesie edita et usitata, canonice instituimus, ipsumque in corporalem possessionem dicte vicarie induximus, cum suis juribus et pertinenciis universis In cuius rei testimonium sigillum nostrum presentibus est appensum. Datum in domo nostro capitulari x° die Februarii ....

---

* See note on *solveret*, p. 88.

† See *fero* in Word List.

‡ *solveret, esset*: subjunctives after the command.

And the other witness, John Broun, being sworn,* deposed that he went across (lit., made the crossing) to the house of the said Agnes, and took with him R. B., in order that he might hear (imperf. subj.—to express purpose) the communication held between them, whereupon, he himself, finding her at home, sought from her the sum of 2s, which she owed to Henry Pyper. She gave reply that she would pay the same sum at the feasts, namely of the Purification (of Blessed Mary) and the remaining part of the sum at the feast of the Visitation (of Blessed Mary)

The opposing party sought a day to object to the evidence (lit., words) of the witnesses. She had Wednesday next following, on which she neither appeared in person nor by proctor, whereupon she was suspended because of her contumacy, and Wednesday next following the feast of St. Thomas was assigned to the parties to hear the final sentence.

The parties (being) present (abl. absolute) sentence was passed in this form: That A. C. should pay 3s 4d, namely at 2 feasts; the first payment should be on the feast of the Assumption (of Blessed Mary), namely 20d, the second payment on the feast of St. Michael, namely 20d; and indeed she took her corporal oath to make this payment faithfully (lit., to make which payment indeed).

An Institution and Induction

To all Christ's faithful be it manifest by (these) presents that we, the Chapter of the collegiate church of W., of the diocese of ...., have canonically admitted (*canonice admisimus*) Master John Piers, priest of the said diocese, to the vicarage of the canonry and prebend of Wessle in the said church of W., vacant (*vacantem*) by the death of Master Thomas Lambe, chaplain, the last vicar of the same, upon the presentation of Master William Manne, canon of the said church and prebendary of the aforesaid prebend of Wessle in the same, truly patron of the same vicarage, and the same Master John Piers we have canonically instituted perpetual vicar in the form of ordination prescribed and used upon admission of vicars of the said church and we have inducted him into corporal possession of the said vicarage with all its rights and appurtenances. In testimony of which our seal is appended to these presents. Given in our Chapter house on the 10th day of February.....

* Past participle, lit., 'having been sworn'.

Some Items from Bishops' Registers

A Presentation

Venerabili in Christo domino Johanni, Dei gratia .... *episcopo, devotus suus in Christo filius Adam de Kele, salutem, reverenciam, et honorem. Ad ecclesiam de Tottingham, vestre diocesis, per mortem Ricardi de Teynton, nuper eiusdem ecclesie rectoris, vacantem et ad meam presentacionem spectantem, dilectum mihi in Christo Ricardum de Stoke, clericum, sancte paternitati vestre presento, supplicans quod predictum Ricardum ad eandem ecclesiam admittere et ipsum in eadem instituere velitis* (pres. subj. of *volo*) *intuitu caritatis. Data apud Kirby quarto die* .... *Valeat paternitas vestra semper in domino.*

Inquisition before Institution

Johannes miseracione divina .... *episcopus, dilecto in Christo filio magistro W., officiali suo, salutem, gratiam, et benedictionem. Presentavit nobis Adam de Kele, dilectum clericum suum Ricardum de Stoke, presbiterum, ad ecclesiam de Tottingham, nostre diocesis, vacantem, ut dicitur, per mortem Ricardi de T., nuper eiusdem ecclesie rectoris, et ad presentationem suam spectantem. Quocirca vobis mandamus quatinus, convocatis rectoribus et vicariis decanatus loci, diligenter in pleno capitulo faciatis* (pres. subj.—after the command) *inquiri* (pres. infin. passive) *si dicta ecclesia vacat, qualiter vacat, a quo tempore vacavit, quantumque valeat; si est litigiosa vel pensionaria, et cui, et in quantum; quis verus patronus eiusdem et quis ad eandem ecclesiam, tempore pacis, ultimo presentavit; de moribus presentati, de literatura, ordinibus, et etate, ac aliis articulis debitis et consuetis. Facta vero inquisicione eam nobis sub sigillis eorum per quos facta fuerit, et sigillo nostro inclusam modo quo convenit transmittatis.*

Some Items from Bishops' Registers

A Presentation

To the venerable in Christ Lord John, by God's grace, Bishop (of ....), his devoted son in Christ, Adam de Kele (gives) greeting, reverence and honour. For the church of T., of your diocese, being vacant by the death of R. de T., lately rector of the same church, and belonging to my presentation, I present my beloved in Christ, R. de S., clerk, to your holy Fatherhood, beseeching that of (lit., in respect of) your charity you may be willing to admit the aforesaid R. to the same church and to institute him therein (lit., in the same). Given at K. on the 4th day .... May your Fatherhood ever prosper in the Lord.

Inquisition before Institution

John, by divine mercy, Bishop (of ....), to (his) beloved son in Christ, Master W., his Official, greeting, grace and blessing. To us has Adam de K. presented his beloved clerk R. de S., priest, for the church of T., of our diocese, (it) being vacant, as it is said, by the death of R. de T., lately rector of the same church, and belonging to his presentation. Wherefore we command you that, having called together the rectors and vicars (abl. absol.—lit., the rectors and vicars having been called together) of the local deanery (lit., deanery of the place), you should cause inquiry diligently to be made (lit., it to be inquired) in full chapter* if the said church is vacant, in what manner it is vacant, from what time it has been vacant, and how much it may be worth; if it is subject to dispute, or charged with a pension, and to whom and to what amount; who is the true patron of the same and who last, in time of peace, presented to the same church;* of the character of the presented, of his learning, of his orders and age, and other articles due and customary. The inquisition being (lit., having been—abl. absol.) truly made, do you send it (pres. subj.—to express command) in the manner in which it is convenient, to us under the seals of those by whom it has been (lit., shall have been) made, and enclosed with our mandate (lit., sealed document).

... There are a series of 'hidden questions' here, and properly the verbs should be subjunctive; only *valeat* is subjunctive. The scribe regards all the questions as matters of plain fact, except the *value* of the living. This, being dependent on fluctuating tithes, etc., can only be estimated; so there is an unexpressed condition—'if a fair extimate should be made', and *valeat* should be translated as above.

Institution

*J. . . . . . . , episcopus, dilecto sibi in Christo domino Ricardo de Stoke, pres-
bitero, salutem. . . . Ad ecclesiam de T., nostre diocesis, vacantem, ad quam
per Adam de K., verum patronum eiusdem nobis legitime presentatus existis,
te ad eandem admittimus et in eadem canonice rectorem instituimus per presentes. . . .*

Mandate to the Archdeacon to Induct

*J. . . . . . . , episcopus, dilecto in Christo filio, magistro Ricardo, archidiacono
suo, salutem. . . . Quia R. de S., presbiterum, ad ecclesiam de T., ad presentationem Ade de K., intuitu caritatis admisimus, vobis mandamus quatinus
eundem in corporalem possessionem eiusdem ecclesie inducatis et inductum
canonice defendatis. . . .*

A Collation

*Ricardus permissione divina . . . . episcopus, dilecto in Christo filo
magistro Ricardo Cockes utriusque iuris doctori salutem. . . . Ecclesiam paro-
chialem de L. nostrarum collationis et diocesis, per mortem naturalem domini
Johannis Cliffe capellani ultimi Rectoris eiusdem vacantem, tibi conferrimus
intuitu caritatis. Teque Rectorem instituimus canonice in et de eadem cum suis
iuribus et pertinenciis universis; curam animarum parochianorum ipsius ecclesie
tibi in domino plenius committendo, iuribus et consuetudinibus nostris episco-
palibus ac nostra et ecclesie nostre cathedralis . . . . dignitate in omnibus
semper salvis. In cuius rei testimonium . . . . Datum . . . . Anno
domini MlᵐᵒCCC nonagesimo. Et nostre translacionis anno primo. Et consequenter scriptum fuit pro ipsius inductione curato parochie de L. predicte ad
inducendum eundem magistrum Ricardum in forma communi.*

A Resignation

*Venerabili in Christo patri, domino W., Dei gracia . . . . episcopo, suus
devotus clericus R. de Swyndon, salutem, et omnem reverenciam cum honore.
Ecclesiam meam de Wigton, necnon omne ius quod habeo in eadem racione
presentacionis mei facte per dominum Willelmum de Thornton seu admissionis
ad eandem, in vestre sanctitatis manus, pure, sponte et absolute resigno per
presentes.*

Institution

J. . . . ., Bishop, to his beloved in Christ, Master R. de S., priest, greeting. . . . To the church of T., of our diocese, (it) being vacant, to which thou art lawfully presented to us by A. de K., true patron of the same, we admit thee to the same and canonically institute thee rector in the same by (these) presents. . . .

Mandate to the Archdeacon to Induct

J. . . . ., Bishop, to (his) beloved son in Christ, Master Richard, his Archdeacon, greeting. . . . Whereas of our charity, on the presentation of A. de K., we have admitted R. de S., priest, to the church of T., we command you that you induct* the same into corporal possession of the same church, and that you canonically uphold* him (when so) inducted. . . .

A Collation

R., by divine permission Bishop (of . . . .), to (his) beloved son in Christ, Master Richard C., doctor of both laws (lit., each law), greeting. . . . The parish church of L., of our collation and diocese, being vacant by the natural death of Master J. C., chaplain, the last Rector of the same, in charity we confer on thee. And we canonically institute thee Rector in and of the same, with all its rights and appurtenances; more fully committing† to thee in the Lord, the cure of the souls of the parishioners of the same church, saving ever in all things our episcopal rights and customs, and our dignity and (that) of our cathedral church. In testimony of which . . . . Given . . . . A.D. 1390, and in the first year of our translation. (And subsequently a letter was written [lit., it was written] in common form, for his induction, to the curate of the aforesaid parish of L. to induct the same master R.)

A Resignation

To the venerable father in Christ, Lord W., by God's grace Bishop . . . ., his devoted clerk R. de S. (gives) greeting and all reverence and honour. My church of W., and all right which I have in the same by reason of my presentation (lit., p. of me) made by Master W. de T. or of (my) admission to the same, I resign by (these) presents into your Holiness' hands, purely, voluntarily and absolutely.

---

* Subjunctive of command.
† For improper use of gerund as present participle, see Chapter 22

Letters Dimissory

Ricardus .... *episcopus dilecto nobis in Christo Magistro Nicholao Ryde in legibus Bacallario nostre diocesis salutem.* ... *Ut a quocumque episcopo catholico sedis apostolice graciam et sui executionem officii obtinente ad omnes tam minores quam maiores etiam presbiteratus ordines quos non dum es assecutus licite valeas promoveri. Eo non obstante quod in diocesi nostra oriundus existis dum tamen moribus natalibus et sciencia repertus fueris ydoneus ac ordinatori tuo titulum sufficientem exhibueris aliudque canonicum non obsistat,* liberam tibi recipiendi et cuicumque episcopo huiusmodi memoratos ordines conferendi tenore presentium concedimus facultatem.* ...

A Commendation

XVI Kalendas Marcii manavit littera sub hac forma. J. .... *episcopus dilecto in Christo filio Thome de Norton, diacono, salutem.* ... *Ecclesiam de Crossegates, nostre diocesis, ad quam te asseris legitime presentatum, ob utilitatem ipsius ecclesie et ut animarum periculo salubrius consulatur* (pres. subj. passive, of *purpose*), *tibi duximus commendandam.*

Licence to Study

C. ...., *episcopus, dilecto in Christo filio Matheo de Stanton Rectori ecclesie de A. nostre diocesis, salutem.* ... *Laudabile propositum quod ad studendum ut asseris intime concepisti favore gracie specialis prosequi cupientes, ut fructum in ecclesia Dei tuo tempore afferre valeas opportunum, ut per triennium continuum a data presentium proxime numerandum literarum studio congruo et honesto licite valeas†* *insistere ubicumque viget studium generale infra regnum Anglie tenore presentium libere dispensamus, proviso tamen quod dicte ecclesie tue medio tempore deserviatur laudabiliter in divinis et quod interim in eadem idoneum responsalem habeas loco tui.* ...

---

* See note on Inquisition before Institution (*valeat*): here, the unexpressed condition is 'if there should be any', i.e., other objection, according to Canon Law.
    † Subjunctive of purpose.

Letters Dimissory

R........, Bishop, to our beloved in Christ Master N. R., of our diocese, Bachelor of Laws, greeting. . . . That—by whatsoever catholic bishop, maintaining the grace of the apostolic see and the execution of his office,—thou mayst* lawfully have power to be promoted to all orders of the priesthood both minor and major also, to which thou hast not yet attained. Notwithstanding (abl. absol.—it notwithstanding) that thou dost originate in our diocese, yet, provided that in native character and in learning thou shalt have been found suitable, and shall have shown sufficient title to thy ordainer, and that there be no other canonical impediment (lit., and that other canonical thing may not obstruct), we grant to thee by the tenor of these presents, free sanction to receive (lit., of receiving), and to whatsoever bishop, to confer (lit., of conferring) orders of the kind mentioned. . . .

A Commendation

On XVI Kalends of March a letter issued in this form: J........, Bishop, to his beloved son in Christ, T. de N., deacon, greeting. . . . The church of C., of our diocese, to which thou declarest thyself lawfully presented, we have thought fit should be commended to thee (gerundive—to-be-commended, agreeing with *ecclesiam*), to the advantage of the church itself, and that more wholesome provision may be made against the peril of the souls (lit., that it may be more healthily provided against the peril).

Licence to Study

C......, Bishop, to his beloved son in Christ, M. de S., Rector of the church of A., of our diocese, greeting. . . . Desiring (*cupientes*, i.e., the Bishop, speaking of himself as 'we') to pursue, by favour of special grace, the laudable plan, which, as thou dost assert, thou hast deeply conceived for study (lit., studying), so that thou mayst in thy time be able to bear seasonable fruit in the church of God, we freely grant dispensation by the tenor of these presents that thou mayst lawfully be able to apply thyself to a fitting and honourable study of letters, for three years continuous, to-be-reckoned next from the date of these presents, wherever a university flourishes within the realm of England, yet provided that in the meantime thy said church be laudably served (lit., it be served to) in (the matter of) divine service, and that meanwhile thou hast a suitable representative in the same in place of thyself. . . .

* Present subjunctive of purpose.

WORD LIST
Preface

Medieval Latin continues to employ many classical words, and while Baxter and Johnson's *Medieval Latin Word-List*★ is a reliable book of reference for medieval vocabulary, it does not include classical words, such as a student distrustful of his school Latin might want to look up. Classical Latin dictionaries on the other hand include only a small proportion of medievalisms.

This word list, therefore, attempts to provide in one work of reference both the classical and medieval vocabulary met with in a study of medieval documents. A large number of such documents has been analysed for vocabulary and idiom; quite soon it was obvious that while they make use of common form, they nevertheless tend to show endless small individualities or peculiarities of vocabulary, spelling, or phrasing, and to cover all possible contingencies would demand a very much longer word list. This list, then, is intended as a bridge leading to a later use of the *Medieval Latin Word-List* and a good classical dictionary.

An attempt has been made to help weak Latin scholars and complete beginners by showing fully the genitive forms of nouns where they are likely to cause difficulty, by indicating the forms and declension of some of the more common Christian names met with, by giving separately in their proper alphabetical order some of the more difficult comparatives and superlatives of adverbs and adjectives and also some of the more difficult participles of verbs, and by giving fully the perfect tenses of verbs where there may be a possibility of doubt in the student's mind.

Students should note that the letters *c* and *t* are often indistinguishable from each other in medieval documents, and often *c* tends to take the place of the classical *t*, as in words like *locacio* for *locatio*. The letters *u* and *v* are also pretty well interchangeable, as *vnus* for *unus* and *i* and *j* in words like *ius* (*jus*), *iaceo* (*jaceo*), *peius* (*pejus*), *eius* (*ejus*), etc.

Variants in spelling are endless, and where obvious are omitted, as *aysiamentum* for *aisiamentum*.

★ J. H. Baxter, C. Johnson, and P. Abrahams, *Medieval Latin Word-List from British and Irish Sources*, 2nd ed., Oxford, 1935.

How to determine declension of nouns and adjectives from the Word List

1st declension (-*e* genitive)

   pastura, -e (f.)—pasture
   persona, -e (m.)—a parson

2nd declension (-*i* genitive)

   dominus, -i (m.)—a lord
   pratum, -i (n.)—a meadow
   messuagium, -ii (n.)—a messuage
   faber, -bri (m.)—a smith
   armiger, -eri (m.)—an esquire

Adjectives of 1st and 2nd declensions

   predictus, -a, -um (adj.)—aforesaid
   noster, -tra, -trum (adj.)—our
   liber, -era, -erum (adj.)—free

3rd-declension nouns (-*is* genitive)

   pater, -tris (m.)—father
   libertas, -tatis (f.)—liberty
   corpus, -oris (n.)—body

3rd-declension adjectives

1. Masculine and feminine form the same, separate form for neuter,
    (m.f.) (n.)
   e.g., *omnis, -e* (adj.)—all
   i.e., only nominative singular given.
2. Same form for all genders: then nominative singular and genitive
    (m.f.n.) (gen.)
   given, e.g., *presens, -entis* (adj.)—present.

4th declension (-*us* genitive)

   visus, -us (m.)—view
   domus, -us (f.)—house

5th declension (-*ei* genitive)

   dies, diei (m. or f.)—day
   res, rei (f.)—thing

Select Word List for the Reading of Local Historical Records

---

a, ab, abs (prep. with abl.)—from, by

abbas, abbatis (m.)—abbot

abbatia, -ie (f.)—abbey

abbutto (1)—to border upon, adjoin

abduco, -ere, -duxi, -ductum (3)—to lead away, remove

abinde (adv.)—thenceforward, thereafter

abjuro (1)—to renounce by oath

absolute (adv.)—entirely

absolutio, -ionis (f.)—absolution (eccles.)

absque (prep. with abl.)—without

absum, abesse, afui—to be away from, absent, lacking

ac, atque (conj.)—and

accido, -ere, accidi (3)—to occur, happen; to fall due

accipio, -ere, -cepi, -ceptum (3)—to take, receive, accept, take possession of

accipiter, -tris (m.)—a hawk

accommodo (1)—to accommodate, comply with; to lend

accresco, -ere, -crevi, -cretum (3)—to increase; to aggravate excommunication (eccles.)

acquietantia, -ie (f.)—quittance, discharge

acquietantialis, -e (adj.)—of, or for, a quittance

acquieto (1)—to quit, discharge

acra, -e (f.)—an acre; an acre strip

actio, -ionis (f.)—action, especially legal action

ad (prep. with acc.)—towards, to, at, for

    ad festum—at the feast

    ad opus—for the use or benefit of

    ad valens; ad valentiam; ad valorem—to the value of

Adam, Adam, Ade, Ade, Ada (m.)—Adam

addo, -ere, -didi, -ditum (3)—to add

adhuc (adv.)—thus far, hitherto, as yet, still

adiacens, -entis (adj.)—bordering on, adjacent to

adinvicem (adv.)—mutually, respectively

adipiscor, -ci, adeptus sum (3, depon.)—to arrive at, reach; to acquire

administrator, -oris (m.), administratrix, -icis (f.)—administrator of property (m., f.)

admissio, -ionis (f.)—admission; induction

admitto, -ere, -misi, -missum (3)—to admit, accept, acknowledge

admoneo, -ere, -monui, -monitum (2)—to advise, admonish; to remind; to claim

adnihilo (1)—to bring to nothing

adnullo (1)—to destroy, annul

adulter, -eri (m.)—adulterer

adultera, -e (f.)—adulteress

adventivus (see dos)

adventus, -us (m.)—Advent; arrival; appearance at court

adversus (adv. and prep.)—opposite, against, towards

advisamentum (see avisamentum)

advocantia, -ie (f.)—advowson; avowry; warranty. Also advocatio, -ionis (f.)

advoco (1)—to claim; to vouch to warranty; to confirm

afferator, -oris (m.)—assessor of fines, affeerer

affero, afferre, attuli, allatum (3)—to bear, bring

affido (1)—to declare on oath

affrus (see *averus*)

aggravatus, -a, -um (adj.)—in a state of aggravated excommunication (eccles.)

agistamentum, -i (n.)—agistment, dues paid for same

Agnes, Agnetis (f.)—Agnes

agnus, -i (m.)—a lamb

ago, -ere, egi, actum (3)—to act, to do

aisiamentum, -i (n.)—easement

alba, -e (f.)—alb; white linen cloth

albacio, -ionis (f.)—white-washing

albus, -a, -um (adj.)—white; whitened; blank

alias (adv.)—at another time; elsewhere; otherwise; alias

alicubi (adv.)—somewhere, anywhere

alieno (1)—to alienate, to transfer by sale

aliquando (adv.)—at some time, at any time

aliquis, aliquid (pron.)—someone, something; anyone, anything; (pl.) some, any

alius, alia, aliud (pron. and adj.)—another; other

allegatum, -i (n.)—allegation in eccles. court. Also *allegantia, -ie* (f.)

allocacio, -ionis (f.)—allowance (in accounts)

altare, -is (n., decl. Kennedy, p. 16, §31)—an altar

alter, altera, alterum (adj.)—one (of two), the other (of two)

alteragium, -ii (n.)—alterage. Also *altaragium*

alternatim (adv.)—alternately, by turn; interchangeably

altus, -a, -um (adj.)—high

amerciamentum, -i (n.)—amercement

amercio (1)—to fine, to amerce

amicus, -i (m.)—friend

amitto, -ere, -misi, -missum (3)—to lose; to surrender; to hand over

ammoveo, -ere, -movi, -motum (2)—to remove. Also *amoveo*

amor, -oris (m.)—love; legal compromise

dies amoris—love-day (leg.)

amplifico (1)—to enlarge, increase

amplius (adv.)—besides, further, longer, more

amputo (1)—to lop, cut

Andreas, -am, -ee, -ee, -a (m.)—Andrew

Angli, -orum (m. pl.)—the English

Anglice (adv.)—in English

anima, -e (f.)—spirit, soul

animal, -alis (n., decl. Kennedy, p. 16, §31)—animal, domestic animal

annexo (1)—to annex, to attach to

annexus, -a, -um (past part.)—joined

annoto (1)—to note down

annualis, -e (adj.)—annual

annuatim (adv.)—annually

annuitas, -atis (f.)—annuity

Annunciatio, -ionis (f.)—the Annunciation

annus, -i (m.)—a year

annuus, -a, -um (adj.)—annual

ante (prep. with acc.)—before

ante manum—beforehand

antea (adv.)—formerly

in antea—beforehand; henceforth; for the future

antecessor, -oris (m.), *antecessatrix, -icis* (f.)—ancestor or predecessor (m., f.)

antedictus, -a, -um (adj.)—aforesaid

antiquus, -a, -um (adj.)—old, ancient, senior

ex antiquo—from ancient times, of old

anulus, -i (m.)—a ring

aper, apri (m.)—a boar

apostilla, -orum (n.pl.)—'apostles': letters of appeal (to higher eccles. court)

apparens, -entis (adj.)—clear, certain

apparentia, -ie (f.)—appearance in court

appareo, -ere, -ui (2)—to appear in court

apparet—it is clear, it is evident

apparitor, -oris (m.)—apparitor

appello (1)—to call; to appeal; to accuse; to name

appendicium, -ii (n.)—appendage, appurtenance

appendicius, -a, -um (adj.)—appertaining to

appendo, -ere, -pendi, -pensum (3)—to append

appono, -ere, -posui, -positum (3)—to apply something to; to add; to lay a charge; to affix

appono clameum—to lay a claim

appositio, -ionis (f.)—affixing

apprecio (1)—to appraise, to value

approbo (1)—to approve, to prove; to enclose land, to improve or draw benefits from land

appropriator, -oris (m.)—appropriator of a benefice

approprio (1)—to appropriate a benefice

approvamentum, -i (n.)—improvement, or profits from land

appruator, -oris (m.)—one who improves or draws benefit from land

appruo (1)—to enclose land, to improve or draw benefits from land

apud (prep. with acc.)—at, by, near; to, towards

aqua, -e (f.)—water

aquabajulus, -i (m.)—holy-water clerk; parish clerk

aquaticus, -a, -um (adj.)—worked by water

aquilo, -onis (m.)—the north

aquilonaris, -e (adj.)—northern

arabilis, -e (adj.)—arable. Also *arrabilis*

aratrum, -i (n.)—plough, ploughland, measure of land. Also *aretrum*

aratura, -e (f.)—ploughing, ploughservice. Also *arura*

arbitrium, -ii (n.)—judgement

arbor, -oris (f.)—a tree

archidiaconalis, -e (adj.)—archidiaconal

archidiaconatus, -us (m.)—office of archdeacon; archdeaconry

archidiaconus, -i (m.)—archdeacon

arcto (1)—(see *arto*)

area, -e (f.)—hearth

arma, -orum (n.pl.)—arms (heraldic); weapons

armariolum, -i (n.)—cupboard

armiger, -eri (m.)—squire, esquire

aro (1)—to plough

arramio (1) *assisam*—to hold an assize

arrentatio, -ionis (f.)—renting

arrento (1)—to rent

arreragium, -ii (n.)—arrears

articulo (1)—to draw document up in clauses; to article against a person in eccles. court

articulus, -i (m.)—a clause; article

artificium, -ii (n.)—craft-guild; work done by craftsman

arto (1)—to compress, constrict, choke; to draw up in clauses or articles; to restrain, constrain. Also *arcto*

artus, -a, -um (adj.)—strict

arura (see *aratura*)

asporto (1)—to carry off

assalto (1)—to assault

assartum, -i (n.)—forest-clearing, assart. Also *essartum*

assensus, -us (m.)—agreement, assent

assequor, -sequi, -secutus sum (3, depon.)—to pursue

assero, -ere, -serui, -sertum (3)—to claim, declare, assert *assignatus, -i* (m.)—an assign, assignee

assigno (1)—to assign

assisa, -e (f.)—assize; action or claim; tax, charge

assistens, -entis (m.)—assistant; parochial officer

assisus, -a, -um (past part.)—assessed, fixed

assumo, -ere, -sumpsi, -sumptum (3)—to take; to receive

Assumpcio, -ionis (f.)—the Assumption

assurantia, -e (f.)—conveyance (of land)

assuro (1)—to convey (land)

atque (conj.)—and

attachiamentum, -i (n.)—attachment (leg.)

attachio (1)—to attach (leg.)

attestor (1, depon.)—to attest

attinctus, -a, -um (past part.)—attainted

attingo, -ere, -tigi, -tactum (3)—to touch; to reach, arrive at; to border on

attornamentum, -i (n.)—attorneyship, attornment

attornatus, -i (m.)—attorney. Also *attornator, -oris* (m.)

attorno (1)—to depute person to act as attorney

auca, -e (f.)—goose

aucarius, -ii (m.)—gooseherd

audio, -ire, -ivi, -itum (4)—to hear

auditor, -oris (m.)—auditor; a judge of the Court of Audience

aufero, auferre, abstuli, ablatum (3)—to carry away, remove; to rob

aula, -e (f.)—hall, room, house
aula regis—king's court

auster, -tri (m.)—the south

australis, -e (adj.)—southern

aut (conj.)—or

aut . . . aut—either . . . or

autem (conj.)—but, however

autumpnus, -i (m.)—autumn

auxilio (1, with dat.)—to pay feudal aid to; to help

auxilium, -ii (n.)—help; feudal aid; legal aid

ava, -e (f.)—grandmother

avena, -e (f.)—oats, fodder

averium, -ii (n., mostly in pl.)—cattle, livestock. Also *avarium*

averus, -i (m.)—farm-horse or ox. Also *avrus; affrus*

avisamentum, -i (n.)—advice; consideration. Also *advisamentum*

avra, -e (f.)—female draught animal

avus, -i (m.)—grandfather; forefather

bacallarius, -ii (m.)—bachelor

baculum, -i (n.)—stick. Also *baculus, -i* (m.)

baillivus, -i (m.)—bailiff, official. Also *ballivus; ballius*

baptisterium, -ii (n.)—font

baptizatus, -a (past part.)—baptized

barellus, -i (m.)—cask

barganea, -e (f.)—bargain; bargaining

barganizo (1)—to bargain. Also *bargano* (1)

baro, -onis (m.)—baron, great man, tenant-in-chief; burgess

beatus, -a, -um (adj.)—blessed

bedellus, -i (m.)—beadle

bene (adv.)—well, rightly, truly

benedictio, -ionis (f.)—blessing; consecration

beneficio (1)—to present to a benefice (eccles.)

beneficium, -ii (n.)—eccles. benefice; benefit; feudal estate

bercaria, -ie (f.)—sheepfold

bercarius, -ii (m.)—shepherd; sheepfold

bertona, -e (f.)—barton, demesne farm

bestia, -ie (f.)—farm animal; beast of the chase

bidens, -entis (f., gen.pl. -ium)—sheep

billa, -e (f.)—list, bill, notice, receipt; presentments of churchwardens

bis (adv.)—twice

bladum, -i (n., often in pl.)—corn, cornfield

boccus, -i (m., see *bosca*)

bona, -orum (n.pl.)—goods, revenue, income

bonus, -a, -um (adj.)—good

bordarius, -ii (m.)—bordar, tenant

Boreas (m.) (declines as *Andreas*)—the North. Also *Borea; Boria*

borialis, -e (adj.)—northern, north. Also *borealis*

bos, bovis (m., gen.pl. *boum*, dat. and abl.pl. *bobus*)—a bull, ox

bosca, -e (f.)—a wood, firewood
    boccus; boscum; boscus—a wood, woodland

boscallis, -e (adj.)—wooded

bovaria, -e (f.)—a bovate. Also *bovata; boveta*

bovinus, -a, -um (adj.)—of a bull or ox
    caro bovina—beef

bracio (1)—to brew. Also *brasio*

braseum, -ei (n.)—malt. Also *brasium; brasseum*

brecca, -e (f.)—a breach

breve, -is (n.; decl. Kennedy, p. 16, §31)—a writ

brevis, breve (adj.)—short
    infra breve (see *infra*)

brueria, -ie (f.)—heath. Also *bruerium, -ii* (n.); *bruera, -e* (f.)

bruillus, -i (m.)—a wood, covert

brusca, -e (f.)—heath or brushwood

bucellus, -i (m.)—butt, cask

bulla, -e (f.)—a seal

bunda, -e (f.)—bound, boundary

bundans, -antis (pres. part.)—bordering upon

burgagium, -ii (n.)—burgage, property held by burgage-tenure; burgage-tenure

burgensis, -is (m.)—a burgess

burgus, -i (m.)—town, borough

buscellus, -i (m.)—a bushel

butta, -e (f.)—butt of land

cado, -ere, cecidi, casum (3)—to fall
    cadere in—to incur

calumnia, -e (f.)—accusation, charge; challenge; claim. Also *calumpnia; columpnia*

calumnio (1)—to challenge; to claim. Also *calumnior* (1, depon.)

camera, -e (f.)—room, chamber; one-room building; residence; treasury; eccles. law-court, especially when held in private house

camerarius, -ii (m.)—chamberlain

campania, -e (f.)—champion, unenclosed land

campus, -i (m.)—field

cancellum, -i (n.)—chancel

candela, -e (f.)—candle; allowance of candles

canis, -is (m., gen.pl. *-um*)—dog

canon, -onis (m.)—canon

canonicalis, -e (adj.)—canonical

canonicatus, -us (m.)—canonry

canonice (adv.)—canonically

canonicus, -a, -um (adj.)—canonical; canon

cantredum, -i (n.)—cantred, division of land

capella, -e (f.)—chapel

capellanus, -i (m.)—chaplain

capio, -ere, cepi, captum (3)—to take, to rent, to seize, to arrest, to hold a court or inquiry, to receive or exact payments; to hold an eccles. court

capitagium, -ii (n.)—poll-tax. Also *chevagium*

capitalis, -e (adj.)—chief

capitaneus, -ei (m.)—chief pledge of a tithing

capitularis, -e (adj.)—of or for a chapter (eccles.)

capitulum, -i (n.)—chapter, meeting of a chapter

capo, -onis (m.)—a capon

captio, -ionis (f.)—taking, right to take; renting, leasing; rent, lease

capud (see *caput*)

caput, capitis (n.)—head, chief; headland

  in capite—in chief, chiefly

  ex capite—of one's own accord

  per capita—per head (i.e., poll-tax, taking into account each person)

caputium, -ii (n.)—hood; academic hood

carbo, -onis (m.)—coal

carco (1)—to load

carecarius, -ii (m.)—carter; ploughman

carecta, -e (f.)—cart, cartload. Also *carectata; carrata*

careo (2)—to lack

cariagium, -ii (n.)—carting, carriage, carriageway; right of carriageway

cario (1)—to carry, cart

caritas, -tatis (f.)—charity; monastic allowance of food

caritativus, -a, -um (adj.)—charitable

carnifex, -icis (m.)—a butcher

caro, carnis (f.)—flesh

carrata (see *carecta*)

carruca, -e (f.)—plough, plough-team, carucate. Also *carrucata; carucata*

carta, -e (f.)—charter, deed

caseus, -i (m.), *caseum* (n.)—cheese

casso (1)—to quash. Also *quasso*

castigo (1)—to punish, chastise

casus, -us (m.)—chance, accident; case, suit

catallum, -i (n.)—chattel, cattle. Also *catellus, -i* (m.)

cathedra, -e (f.)—chair; bishop's throne

cathedralis, -e (adj.)—of, or for, a cathedral

catholicus, -a, -um (adj.)—Catholic

causa, -e (f.)—legal 'cause'

causatio, -ionis (f.)—plea; objection (leg.)

cautela, -e (f.)—a trick

  ad, per, cautelam—provisionally

cavillatio, -ionis (f.)—cavilling, objection, quibble

cedua (see *silva*)

cedula, -e (f.)—schedule, document, proclamation. Also *schedula*

celebriter (adv.)—solemnly

celebro (1)—to celebrate (Mass), to hold a visitation (bishop's or archdeacon's)

  celebrare concilium, capitulum—to hold a council (eccles.), chapter-meeting

cena, -e (f.)—supper

censeo, -ere, censui, censum (2)—to tax, assess, rate, estimate; to resolve; to believe; to consider

centum (indeclin.)—one hundred

cera, -e (f.)—wax

certioro (1)—to inform, apprise; to show

certus, -a, -um (adj.)—fixed, established, certain

cervisia, -e (f.)—beer. Also *cerevisia; cervesia; servisia*

ceteri, -e, -a (pl.)—the others, the rest

charta (see *carta*)

chevagium (see *capitagium*)

chevescia, -e (f.)—headland. Also *chevicium, -ii* (n.)

chirographum, -i (n.)—chirograph. Also *cirographum; cyrographum*

cibum -i (n.)—food

cimiterium, -ii (n.)—cemetery

circa (adv. and prep.)—around, near to, about, nearly

cista, -e (f.)—box, coffin; stew-pond

citatio, -ionis (f.)—citation, summons. Also *citatus, -us* (m.)

cito (1)—to cite, summon

citra (adv. and prep. with accus.)—on this side, on the nearer side; apart from, except; before; since

civis, *-is* (m., gen.pl. *-ium*)—citizen

civitas, *-tatis* (f.)—city, capital city of diocese

clamacium, *-ii* (n.)—claim. Also *clameum*, *-ei* (n.)

clamo (1)—to claim
clamare quietum—to quitclaim

clamor, *-oris* (m.)—claim, complaint, outcry

clarus, *-a*, *-um* (adj.)—clear, net (of accounts)
de claro—net

claudo, *-ere*, *clausi*, *clausum* (3)—to close

clausa, *-e* (f.)—clause

clausula, *-e* (f.)—clause; enclosed place

clausura, *-e* (f.)—close, enclosure, right to enclose, dues paid for same

clausuro (1)—to enclose

clavis, *-is* (f.)—a key

clericus, *-i* (m.)—clerk
c. *pacis*; c. *parochialis*—clerk of the peace; parish clerk

climax, *-acis* (f.)—a stile

cocus, *-i* (m.)—cook

cognomen, *-inis* (n.)—name; nickname

cognosco, *-ere*, *-gnovi*, *cognitum* (3)—to get to know; (in past tenses) to know; to recognize, to admit, to acknowledge

collatio, *-ionis* (f.)—collation (eccles.)

collegiatus, *-a*, *-um* (adj.)—collegiate

colligo, *-ere*, *-legi*, *-lectum* (3)—to gather, collect

colloquium, *-ii* (n.)—a conference

colo, *-ere*, *colui*, *cultum* (3)—to cultivate

columbare, *-is* (n.)—dove-cot

columpnia (see *calumnia*)

comburo, *-ere*, *-bussi*, *-bustum* (3)—burn, burn up, burn lime

comes, *-itis* (m.)—earl

comitatus, *-us* (m.)—county, earldom, county court

comitissa, *-e* (f.)—countess

commater, *-tris* (f.)—godmother. Also *comater*

commendo (1)—to commend to, entrust to

committo, *-ere*, *-misi*, *-missum* (3)—to commit to, entrust to

commoditas, *-atis* (f.)—commodity, product

commodum, *-i* (n.)—opportunity; advantage; profit

commune, *-is* (n., decl. Kennedy, p. 16, §31)—common land, common rights, community, corporation. Also *communia* (n.pl.); *communio*, *-ionis* (f.); *communitas*, *-itatis* (f.) (*communio* also means Holy Communion)

communicacio, *-ionis* (f.)—conversation, communication, intercourse

communico (1)—to have a share in

communis, *-e* (adj.)—common

communo (1)—to have rights of common

commuto (1)—to commute; to commute penance

comparatio, *-ionis* (f.)—presence, appearance

compareo, *-ere*, *-parui*—to be present, appear at court (leg.)

compater, *-tris* (m.)—godfather

compertum est—it was (is) found (by the court) (leg.)

competens, *-entis* (adj.)—suitable, fitting

compleo, *-ere*, *-evi*, *-etum* (2)—to fill up, fulfil, complete

compono, *-ere*, *-posui*, *-positum* (3)—to join, collect, arrange; to compound, to make fine

compos, *-otis* (adj., decl. Kennedy, p. 23, §47)—possessing, in possession of

composicio, -ionis (f.)—composition, payment

compotus, -i (m.)—account, calculation, audit. Also *computus, -i* (m.); *compotum, -i* (n.)

compulsoria, -ie (f.)—an eccles. 'compulsory'

computans, -antis (m.)—accountant

computo (1)—to reckon

concedo, -ere, -cessi, -cessum (3)—to yield, grant, allow

concerno, -ere (3)—to concern, have regard to. Also *conserno*

concessio, -ionis (f.)—grant, concession

concesso (1)—to agree to; to grant

concilium regis—Privy Council

concipio, -ere, -cepi, -ceptum (3)—to comprehend; to conceive

concordia, -ie (f.)—agreement, compromise (leg.)

concordor (1, depon.)—to compromise (leg.), to come to terms

conculco (1)—to trample down

condam (see *quondam*)

condempno (1)—to condemn; to mulct

condicio, -ionis (f.)—condition, stipulation

conditio, -ionis (f.)—founding, foundation, grant

condo, -ere, -didi, -ditum (3)—to put together, construct, found
   c. *testamentum*—to make a will

condono (1)—to grant; to remit, excuse, pardon

conductio, -ionis (f.)—meeting

confectio, -ionis (f.)—a making, completion

confero, -ferre, -tuli, -latum (3)—to confer; to bestow upon

conficio, -ere, -feci, -fectum (3)—to make complete; to consecrate

confirmo (1)—to confirm, strengthen

confiteor, -eri, -fessus sum (2, depon.)—to confess, acknowledge; to do penance

congruenter (adv.)—agreeably, fitly

congruus, -a, -um (adj.)—suitable, fit

conjugata, -e (f.)—married woman

conjuncti fuere—they were married

conjunctim (adv.)—jointly

conqueror, -queri, -questus sum (3, depon.)—to complain

conquestus, -us (m.)—the Conquest; acquisition.

consensus, -us (m.)—agreement, concord

consentio, -ire, -sensi, -sensum (4)—to agree

consequenter (adv.)—subsequently

conservo (1)—to maintain; to keep

considero (1)—to give judgement (leg.)

consilium, -ii (n.)—counsel, advice, counsel (leg. adviser), council

consistorium, -ii (n.)—consistory, an eccles. court, an eccles. assembly

constabularius, -ii (m.)—constable, warden

constare de—to be composed of, consist of

constituo, -ere, -stitui, -stitutum (3)—to fix, establish, appoint, regulate; agree upon, decide

consuesco, -ere, -suevi, -suetum (3)—to accustom, become accustomed

consuetudo, -inis (f.)—custom, usage; customary service or dues; customs duty; customary payment
   c. *Anglie; c. regni*—Common Law

consuetus, -a, -um (adj.)—accustomed

consulitur (with dative; impersonal)—thought-is-taken-for; care-is-taken-against. Also in other tenses and subj.

consulo, -ere, -sului, -sultum (3)—(with acc.) to consult; (with dat.) to take thought for, provide against; to provide for vacant benefice (eccles.)

contento (1)—to satisfy; to pay

contineo, -ere, -tinui, -tentum (2)—to keep together, enclose, restrain, contain

contingens, -entis (adj.)—contingent, conditional

contingo, -ere, -tigi, -tactum (3)—to touch, border on, extend to, appertain to, to befall, come to pass

continuus, -a, -um (adj.)—continuous, successive

contra (adv. and prep. with acc.)—against, before (of time), contrary to

contractio, -ionis (f.)—marriage; marriage-contract

contradicens, -entis (m.)—an opposer of purgation

contradico, -ere, -dixi, -dictum (3)—to refuse

  c. plegium—to refuse to be a pledge or guarantor

contradictio, -ionis (f.)—objection; withdrawal of service

contrarior (1, depon.)—to oppose, be opposed to

contrarius, -a, -um (adj.)—opposite, contrary, opposed

  e contrario; in contrarium—on the other hand

contumacia, -e (f.)—contumacy, disobedience, especially not appearing in eccles. court when ordered

convencio, -ionis (f.)—covenant, agreement. Also *conventio*

convenio, -ire, -veni, -ventum (4)—to meet, assemble; to summon, sue

  convenit—it is agreed; it is fit, suitable, appropriate

conventiono (1)—to covenant, agree

conventus, -us (m.)—convent

convinco, -ere, -vici, -victum (3)—to convict; to prove incontestably

convivium, -ii (n.)—feast

convoco (1)—to call together

cooperta, -e (f.)—married (of a woman)

coopertio, -ionis (f.)—covert (of woods)

coopertor, -oris (m.)—roofer

coopertorium, -ii (n.)—roof, roofing, thatch, cover. Also *coopertura*

copia, -ie (f.)—a copy

copio (1)—to copy

coquina, -e (f.)—kitchen

coram (adv. and prep. with abl.; also with acc.)—in the presence of, before, in front of

cornera, -e (f.)—corner. Also *cornerium, -ii* (n.)

coronarius, -ii (m.)—coroner. Also *coronator, -oris* (m.)

corporalis, -e (adj.)—physical, corporal

corpus, -corporis (n.)—body

corredium, -ii (n.)—gear, possessions, supplies; corrody, allowance of food, maintenance

corrigo, -ere, -rexi, -rectum (3)—to correct, amend

costo (1)—to cost

cotagium, -ii (n.)—cottage

cotarius, -ii (m.)—cottager

cotura, -e (f.)—piece of land

crastinum, -i (n.)—the morrow

  in crastino (with gen.)—on the morrow of (e.g., *in crastino Sancti Hillarii*—the day after the feast of S.H.)

Creatura, -e (f.)—name used in hasty baptism, at a difficult birth, to serve for either sex

credentia, -e (f.)—credit, belief, credence, faith

credo, -ere, -didi, -ditum (3)—(with dat.) to believe, give credence or trust to; (with acc.) to believe, suppose, consider

crementum, -i (n.)—addition of land

crescens, -entis (adj.)—growing

crofta, -e (f.)—croft. Also *croftum, -i* (n.)

croppa, -e (f.)—crop, harvest. Also *croppum, -i* (n.)

crucifixus, -i (m.)—the crucified one, Jesus; crucifix; rood

crux, crucis (f.)—cross; mark (in documents)

cultellarius, -ii (m.)—cutler

cultura, -e (f.)—piece of cultivated land; furlong

cultellus, -i (m.)—knife

cum (prep. with abl.)—with

cum (conj. with verbs)—when; since; whereas; though (with subj.)

-cum (e.g., *mecum*)—with (e.g., with me)

-cumque (attached to end of word)— -ever (e.g., *quicumque*—whoever; *quandocumque*—whenever)

cunctus, -a, -um (adj., esp. in pl.)—all, the whole

cupio, -ere, -ivi, -itum (3)—to desire

cura, -e (f.)—care; cure of souls (eccles.)

curatus, -i (m.)—priest having care of souls, curate

curia, -e (f.)—court of law; King's court; court-yard

curo (1)—to care for, take care of, take care that

curro, -ere, cucurri, cursum (3)—to run, to flow; to be current

curtilagium, -ii (n.)—courtyard, yard, curtilage

custodia, -ie (f.)—custody; tenure of land; wardship of minors

custodio (4)—to protect, keep, preserve

custos, -odis (m.)—keeper, warden, guardian

custuma, -e (f.)—customary payment

custumarius, -ii (m.)—customary tenant

custus, -us (m.)—cost, expense

cyra (see *scyra*)

cyrographum (see *chirographum*)

damnum, -i (n.)—loss, damage; pl.— damages, compensation. Also *dampnum*

dans, -antis (pres. part. of *do*)—giving

data, -e (f.), *datum, -i* (n.), *datus, -i* (m.)—date

datus, -a, -um (past part.)—given; dated

Davidus, -i (m.)—David

de (prep. with abl.)—of, from

　de cetero—henceforth

　de consensu—with the consent of

　de futuro—in the future

　de longe—from afar

　de novo—newly

　de pari—on equal footing

　de post—behind

　de post facto—afterwards

　de presenti—at present

　de prope—near

　de ultra—on the farther side of

　de versus—in front of; away from

debeo (2)—I owe, I ought, I must, I should; (with infinitive) I am obliged, bound (to do something)

debiter (adv.)—duly

debitor, -oris (m.)—debtor

debitum, -i (n.)—debt

　d. principale—principal sum of a debt

debitus, -a, -um (past part.)—owed, due

decanatus, -us (m.)—deanery

decanus, -i (m.)—dean

decasus, -us (m.)—diminution, loss, decay

decedo, -ere, -cessi, -cessum (3)—to withdraw, depart, die

decem (indeclinable)—ten

decenna, -e (f.)—tithing. Also *dicena; disena; dissena*

decennarius, -ii (m.)—tithing-man

decensus (see *descensus*)

decessus, -us (m.)—lease, demise; death

decies (adv.)—ten times

decima, -e (f.)—tithe; tenth (paid by incumbents)

decimo (1)—to pay or exact tithe

decimus, -a, -um (adj.)—tenth

decipio, -ere, -cepi, -ceptum (3)—to deceive, cheat

decollacio, -ionis (f.)—beheading

decresco, -ere, -crevi, -cretum (3)—to decrease

dedico (1)—to assert; to deny

deduco, -ere, -duxi, -ductum (3)—to subtract; to bring to trial; to exempt

defalta, -e (f.)—default, defection; deduction, withholding

defamatrix, -cis (f.)—defamer (female)

defamo (1)—to defame, to accuse

defectus, -us (m.)—default, defect; deduction, withholding

defendens, -entis (m., f.)—defendant

defendo, -ere, -di, -sum (3)—to repel, ward off, defend, uphold, oppose, forbid; to maintain or hold land, to enclose or fence land; (with *se*) to be assessed at

defensio, -ionis (f.)—prohibition

defensor, -oris (m.)—defendant; counsel (leg.); defender

defensum, -i (n.)—defence; enclosure; prohibition. Also *defensus, -us* (m.)

deffinio (4)—to define, determine. Also *diffinio*

deficio, -ere, -feci, -fectum (3)—to be wanting, to fail, default

deforciamentum, -i (n.)—deforcement. Also *difforciatio, -ionis* (f.)

deforcians, -iantis (m., f.)—deforcer, deforciant. Also *deforciator, -oris* (m.)

deforcio (1)—to deforce

defunctus, -a, -um (past part.)—dead, deceased

deinceps (adv.)—next

deinde (adv.)—thereafter, then, next

delatio, -ionis (f.)—delay. Also *dilatio*

deliberatio, -ionis (f.)—delivering, delivery

delibero (1)—to deliver. Also *delivero*

delinquo, -ere, -liqui, -lictum (3)—to do wrong, trespass, offend

delivero (see *delibero*)

demanda, -e (f.)—demand, claim

demando (1)—to demand, claim

demissio (see *dimissio*)

denarata, -e (f.)—pennyworth

denarius, -ii (m.)—coin, penny, money

deparcacio, -ionis (f.)—pound-breaking

deparco (1)—to break pound

depono, -ere, -posui, -positum (3)—to put down; to state as evidence, to depose (leg.)

deprivatio, -ionis (f.)—deprivation (eccles.); deposition (leg.)

deputo (1)—to appoint, depute, entrust

descendo, -ere, -di, -sum (3)—to go down, descend; to descend (of rights or property)

descensus, -us (m.)—descent. Also *discensus, -us* (m.); *decensus, -us* (m.)

deservio (4)—to serve; to earn or merit; to officiate in eccles. capacity, to 'serve' a parish

despectio, -ionis (f.)—contempt

destruens, -entis (m., f.)—a destroyer

destruo, -ere, -struxi, -structum (3)—to destroy

detineo (2)—to detain, keep back

Deus, -i (m.)—God

devenio, -ire, -veni, -ventum (4)—to go to, to reach, to become

devotio, -ionis (f.)—a dedicating, a pious donating

devotus, -a, -um (adj.)—devoted, dedicated

dexter, -tra, -trum (adj.)—right (as opposed to left)

diatim (adv.)—daily, day by day

dico, -ere, dixi, dictum (3)—to say; to declare formally, espec. in eccles. court *dictum, -i* (n.)—word, saying; formal declaration

dictus, -a, -um (adj.)—said, aforesaid; called

dies, diei (generally m., but sometimes f.)—day, time, lifetime, day appointed for appearance in court

dies amoris—love-day (leg.)

dies dominica—Sunday

dies Iovis—Thursday

dies Iovis absolutionis—Maundy Thursday

dies Lune—Monday

dies Martis—Tuesday

dies Mercurii—Wednesday

dies Solis—Sunday

dies Veneris—Friday

dies Veneris Sanctus—Good Friday

dies Veneris Parasceves—Good Friday

dies Wodenis—Wednesday

dieta, -e (f.)—a day, day's journey, day's work, measure of land

difficilis, -e (adj.)—difficult

diffinitivus, -a, -um (adj.)—definite, final

difforciatio (see *deforciamentum*)

dignitas, -tatis (f.)—dignity

dignus, -a, -um (adj.)—worthy, deserving; qualified (for rank, status, etc.)

dilectus, -a, -um (adj.)—beloved

diligenter (adv.)—diligently

dimidia, -e (f.)—half

dimidius, -a, -um (adj.)—half

dimissio, -ionis (f.)—handing over, demise. Also *demissio, -ionis* (f.)

dimissiones, -um (f. pl.)—fees for dismissal from an eccles. case

dimitto, -ere, -misi, -missum (3)—to demise

diocesis, -is (f.)—diocese. Also *diocesa, -e* (f.)

discedo, -ere, -cessi, -cessum (3)—to die; depart

discensus (see *descensus*)

discessus, -us (m.)—death

disciplina, -e (f.)—discipline, penance

disco, -ere, didici (3)—to learn

dispensator, -oris (m.)—treasurer, bursar, steward

dispenso (1)—to grant dispensation

dispersono (1)—to disparage, abuse

disponso (1)—to betroth

dissasio (see *disseiso*)

disseisina, -e (f.)—disseisin

disseisitrix, -icis (f.)—female disseisor

disseiso (1)—to disseise. Also *dissasio* (1)

dissensio, -ionis (f.)—disagreement, dispute

dissimilis, -e (adj.)—unlike

dissonus, -a, -um (adj.)—unfit

disto, -are (1)—to stand apart, be separate, distant

se distare—to be separated

districtio, -ionis (f.)—distress, distraint

districtum, -i (n.)—thing taken in distraint

districtus, -i (m.)—territory, district

distringo, -ere, -nxi, -ctum (3)—to distrain

distructio, -ionis (f.)—damage, destruction. Also *distruxio*

diu (adv.)—for a long time, long since

diutissime (adv.)—longest

diutius (adv.)—longer

diversim (adv.)—in different directions, separately, severally

diversimodo (adv.)—in various ways

diversimodus, -a, -um (adj.)—of various kinds

diversus, -a, -um (adj.)—diverse, various

diverticulum, -i (n.)—a by-way

divina, -orum (n. pl.)—divine service

divinus, -a, -um (adj.)—divine

divisa, -e (f.)—boundary, boundary mark, dividing; court, or court-day (leg.). Also *divisum, -i* (n.)

divisim (adv.)—separately

divisio, -ionis (f.)—piece of land

divus, -a, -um (adj.)—blessed, saint

do, dare, dedi, datum (1)—to give, grant; give in marriage

    dare ad remanentiam—to grant a reversionary right

    dare de fine—to pay a fine

    dare in manu—to pledge

    dare intellegi—to give to understand

doageria, -e (f.)—dowager

doarium, -ii (n.)—dower or dowry. Also *dodarium, -ii* (n.)

doctor, -oris (m.)—doctor

dolium, -ii (n.)—cask, jar, tun

dolus, -i (m.)—fraud, deceit

domanicum, -i (n.)—demesne land. Also *domanium, -ii* (n.); *dominicum, dominium*

domicellus (m.), *domicella* (f.)—servant (m. or f.)

domicilium, -ii (n., see *domus*)

domina, -e (f.)—Lady

Dominica, -e (f.)—Sunday

dominicalis, -e (adj.)—of the Lord, of or for Sunday, of a lord, for a lord; demesne

dominicus, -a, -um (adj.)—of or for a lord; demesne

dominium (see *domanicum*)

dominus, -i (m.)—lord, the Lord; courtesy title for cleric without degree, Sir, Master

    domnus, -i (m.), or *dompnus, -i* (m.) —lord

domus, -us (f.)—house, home, room, religious house. Also *domicilium*

domus hostium—guest house of monastery

donarium, -ii (n.)—gift; grant. Also *donatio, -ionis* (f.); *donatum, -i* (n.)

    donum, -i (n.)—gift, giving (of bride)

    de dono—as a gift

dos, dotis (f.)—dowry, endowment, widow's dower; eccles. endowment

dos adventiva—dowry given by other than father of bride

dos perfectiva—dowry given by father or grandfather of bride

dotabilis, -e (adj.)—entitled to dower

dotaria, -e (f.)—dowager

dotarium, -ii (n.)—widow's dower, dowry

dotatio, -ionis (f.)—dowry, endowment

doto (1)—to endow; to dower

dragium, -ii (n.)—drage, mixed corn. Also *dragetum, -i* (n.)

duarium, -ii (n.)—widow's dower; dowry

ducenti, -e, -a—two hundred

duco, -ere, duxi, ductum (3)—to lead, to take as husband or wife; to consider, to convene, to think fit to; to cause

    ducere dignum—to approve

    ducere sectam—to produce witnesses

dudum (adv.)—a short time ago; before, formerly

dum (conj.)—whilst; as long as; until; (with subj.)—provided that

dumtaxat (adv.)—to this extent, so far, only; at least

duo, due, duo—two

duodecim—twelve

duodecimus, -a, -um (adj.)—twelfth

duodetricensimus, -a, -um (adj.)—twenty-eighth

duodetriginta—twenty-eight

duodevicensimus, -a, -um (adj.)—eighteenth

duodeviginti—eighteen

duratio, -ionis (f.)—duration

duro (1)—to last, to extend, to stretch

e (see *ex*)

ecclesia, -e (f.)—church; body of church as distinct from chancel

eciam (see *etiam*)

ed (for *et*)—and

edificium, -ii (n.)—building

edifico (1)—to build

editus, -a, -um (past part.)—proclaimed, ordained

effectus, -us (m.)—effect, tendency, purpose

eger, egra, egrum (adj.)—ill, sick

ego, egomet, egometipse—I, I myself (dative often *michi*)

elapsus, -a, -um (past part.)—elapsed, past

elemosina, -e (f.)—alms

elemosino (1)—to grant in alms

elevo (1)—to raise, lift

eligo, -ere, -legi, -lectum (3)—to choose, to elect

emenda, -e (f.)—fine, compensation

emendatio, -ionis (f.)—fine, compensation, improvement, repair

emendo (1)—to pay a fine, compensate, make amends; to repair

emo, emere, emi, emptum (3)—to buy

eo, ire, ivi, itum (4)—to go

episcopalis, -e (adj.)—episcopal

episcopus, -i (m.)—bishop

equalis, -e (adj.)—equal

equaliter (adv.)—equally, in equal parts

equinus, -a, -um (adj.)—worked by horse-power

equito (1)—to ride

equus, -a, -um (adj.)—even, level, equal

equus, -i (m.); *equa, -e* (f.)—horse; mare

eradico (1)—to uproot

erigo, -ere, erexi, erectum (3)—to erect

erronice (adv.)—wrongly, in error

escaeta, -e (f.)—escheat

escambio (1)—to exchange. Also *excambio* (1)

escambium, -ii (n.) or, *excambium, -ii* (n.)—exchange

escuro (1)—to scour

essartum (see *assartum*)

esse (see *sum*)—to be

essendum, -i (n.)—(gerund of *esse*) being

essiamentum (for *aisiamentum*)

essonia, -ie (f.)—essoin

essonio (1)—to essoin

esterium (see *strekum*)

estimatio, -ionis (f.)—reckoning, valuation

estoverium, -ii (n.)—estover, allowance of wood

estreca (see *strekum*)

et (conj.)—and

et . . . et—both . . . and

et (in place of *etiam*)—also, even

etas, -atis (f.)—age

etiam (conj.)—also, furthermore, even

etiamsi—even if, although

euntis (see *iens*)

evacuo (1)—to make void, to cancel

evangelia, -orum (n.pl.)—book containing the Gospels

evenio, -ire, -veni, -ventum (4)—to come forth, come to pass; to happen, result

ex (often *e* before a consonant; prep. with abl.)—from; out of; according to; as a result of

e converso—conversely

ex adverso—adversely

ex nunc—hereafter

ex opposito—opposite

ex quo—since, inasmuch as

ex tunc—thereafter

exactio, -ionis (f.)—charge; accusation (leg.); demand; tax; calling in of debts

Exaltatio, -ionis (f.)—a raising-up; Exaltation (of the Holy Cross)

excambio (see *escambio*)

excambium (see *escambium*)

excessus, -us (m.)—excess, surplus

excipio, -ere, -cepi, -ceptum (3)—to take out, withdraw, exempt, to except; to take, receive; to support, sustain excludo, -ere, -clusi, -clusum (3)—to exclude; to remove

excommunicatio, -ionis (f.)—excommunication

executio, -ionis (f.)—execution

executor, -oris (m.)—administrator, executor

executrix -icis (f.)—executrix

exemplo (1)—to make a copy of a document. Also exemplifico (1)

exemplum, -i (n.)—transcript, copy

exeo, -ire, exivi or exii, exitum (4)—to go out, issue from, be derived from

exerceo (2)—to exercise

exhibeo (2)—to present, deliver, maintain, support, provide for, show

exiens, exeuntis (pres. part. of exeo)—issuing from

exigenda (n.pl.)—exigent, first step in outlawry (leg.)

exigentia, -e (f.)—necessity, demand

exigo, -ere, exegi, exactum (3)—to demand, enforce

existens, -entis (pres. part.)—existing

existo, -ere, -stiti, -stitum (3)—to exist, to be; used for esse, e.g.:

e. oriundus—I am born, sprung from

e. presentatus—I am presented

existit commissum—it is commissioned

exitus, -us (m.)—exit, revenue, profits, issue, offspring

exoneratio, -ionis (f.)—discharge, exoneration

exonero (1)—to discharge, to free

exorior, exoriri, exortus (3 and 4)—to come forth, arise, begin to speak

expedio (4)—to set free, expedite, despatch

expeditio, -ionis (f.)—expedition

expendo, -ere, -di, -sum (3)—to pay out, to expend

expensum, -i (n.)—payment, money paid

expiratio, -ionis (f.)—expiry, end

expostulo (1)—to demand, require; find fault with

exsto, -stare, -steti, -statum (1)—to stand out; to survive, remain, exist

extendens, -entis (adj.)—extending

extendo, -ere, -tendi, -tentum (3)—to stretch out, extend, to survey; to value

extendor, -oris (m.)—surveyor, valuer

extenta, -e (f.)—extent, survey, valuation

extentator, -oris (m.)—official executing a writ of extent

extra (adv. and prep.)—on the outside, without, besides, beyond, except

extracta, -e (f.)—estreat; copy; removal. Also extractus

extrahura, -e (f.)—a stray

extraneus, -a, -um (adj., also used as noun)—stranger, foreign

faba, -e (f.)—bean

faber, fabri (m.)—smith

fabrica, -e (f.)—fabric, especially of church; fabric-fund; workshop; building

facilis, -e (adj.)—easy

facio, -ere, feci, factum (3)—to do; to act; to make; (with infin.) to cause

facere homagium—to pay homage

facere pro—to give a verdict in favour of (leg.)

factura, -e (f.)—a making

factus, -a, -um (past part.)—made

facultas, -tatis (f.)—opportunity; sanction; faculty of a university

falcatio, -ionis (f.)—mowing

falco (1)—to mow

falso (adv.)—falsely

falx, falcis (f.)—a scythe

famo (1)—to defame

farina, -e (f.)—flour

fasces, -ium (m.pl.)—faggots

fasciculi, -orum (m.pl.)—faggots

fateor, -eri, fassus sum (2)—to confess, acknowledge

favor, -oris (m.)—favour

femina, -e (f.)—wife, woman

fenum, -i (n.)—hay

feodarius, -ii (m.)—feudal tenant; feodary

feodator, -oris (m.)—vassal, feudal tenant. Also *feudalis, -is* (m.)

feoditas, -tatis (f.)—fealty

feodo (1)—to enfeoff

feodotalis, -is (f.)—fealty, feudal service

feodum (n.)—fief, fee. Also *feodus, -i* (m.); *feudum, -i* (n.); *feudus, -i* (m.)

feoffamentum, -i (n.)—feoffment

feoffatus, -i (m.)—feoffee

feoffo (1)—to enfeoff

f. in feudum—to enfeoff in fee

fera, -e (f.)—beast of the chase

ferculum, -i (n.)—barrow, dish, course (in a meal)

feretrum, -i (n.)—shrine

feria, -e (f.)—fair

fero, ferre, tuli, latum (3)—to bear, bring

ferrum, -i (n.)—iron; horseshoe; trial by ordeal

festum, -i (n.)—festival, feast

feudalis; feudum (see *feodator; feodum*)

fidejussor, -oris (m.)—one who gives security, surety; godparent

fidelis, -e (adj.)—faithful, faithful subject, vassal

fidelitas, -atis (f.)—fealty

fideliter (adv.)—faithfully

fides, fidei (f.)—faith, fealty, troth

fiducia, -e (f.)—trust, confidence

filia, -e (f.)—daughter

filius, -ii (m.)—son

filius, filia populi—son, daughter, of the people (used of illegitimate children)

filum, -i (n.)—thread

fimum, -i (n.)—dung

finabiliter (adv.)—finally

finalis, -e (adj.)—final

finaliter (adv.)—finally

finio, -ire, -ivi, -itum (4)—to finish; to pay fine

finis, -is (m.; sometimes f.)—end, fine, boundary, limit (gen. pl. *-ium*)

fio, fieri, factus sum (3, passive of *facio*)—to be made, to become

firma, -e (f.)—farm, rent, fixed payment

firmarius, -ii (m.)—farmer, renter

firmitas, -atis (f.)—strength, firmness, stability

firmiter (adv.)—firmly

firmo (1)—to farm; to farm out

firmus, -a, -um (adj.)—stable, steadfast, firm

flagello (1)—to whip; to thresh

focale, -is (n.)—fuel; (in pl.) firewood

fodiator, -oris (m.)—digger

fodio, -ere, fodi, fossum (3)—to dig

fons, fontis (m., gen. pl. *-ium*)—spring, fountain, source

forarium, -ii (n.)—headland. Also *forera, -e* (f.)

fore—future infinitive of *esse*

forinsecus (adv.)—on the outside, external, foreign

forinsecus, -a, -um (adj.)—forinsec, external, foreign

forinsecus, -i (m.)—person living outside a city

forisfacio, -ere, -feci, -factum (3)—to do wrong, forfeit, pay or incur forfeiture

forisfactum, -i (n.)—damage, injury, forfeiture, penalty

forisfactura, -e (f.)—forfeiture, penalty

forma, -e (f.)—form, terms of a document, formula

f. capellae—Chancery form

fortis, -e (adj.)—strong

forum, -i (n.)—market

fossa, -e (f.)—dike, embankment

fossator, -oris (m.)—digger

fossatum, -i (n.)—service of digging, dues paid in lieu; ditch

fossatus -i (m.)—ditch. Also *fossetum, -i* (n.)

fosso (1)—to dig, trench

foveo, -ere, fovi, fotum (2)—to foster, cherish

    f. lenocinium—to indulge in lewdness

franciplegius, -ii (m.)—frankpledge. Also *franciplegium, -ii* (n.)

francus, -a, -um (adj.)—free

frango, -ere, fregi, fractum (3)—to break

frater, fratris (m.)—brother; monk, friar

fraternaliter (adv.)—fraternally

fraus, fraudis (f.)—fraud, injury, detriment, damage

fructus, -us (m.)—fruit

frumentum, -i (n.)—corn, grain

fugo (1)—to drive, to hunt

fui (see *sum*)

fundatio, -ionis (f.)—foundation, endowment (eccles.)

furo (1)—to steal

fustigatio, -ionis (f.)—whipping

fustigo (1)—to whip

futurus, -a, -um (future part., see *sum*)—about-to-be

    in futurum—for the future

gablum, -i (n.)—rent, tax

gallinarium, -ii (n.)—hen-house

galliprelium, -ii (n.)—cock-fighting; cockpit

galo, galonis (m.)—gallon. Also *galona, -e* (f.)

garba, -e (f.)—sheaf of corn

garcio, -ionis (f.)—boy; servant; groom

gardianus, -i (m.)—churchwarden

garilatrix, -icis (f.)—a scold. Also *garrulatrix*

gaudeo, -eri, gavisus sum (2, semideponent)—to use, enjoy the use of, possess

gavisus, -a, -um (past part.)—enjoyed

geldo (1)—to pay geld

geldum, -i (n.)—geld, tax.

generosa, -e (f.)—lady

generosus, -i (m.)—gentleman

gens, gentis (f., gen.pl. *-ium*)—people

gersuma -e (f.)—fine, premium, customary payment; a benevolence

gersumo (1)—to pay a fine, to pay a premium

gigno, -ere, genui, genitum (3)—to beget

gilda, -e (f.)—guild

gora, -e (f.)—gore, triangular piece of land

gracilis, -e (adj.)—lean, slight; meagre

gradus, -us (m.)—step; degree of marriage

gramen, -inis (n.)—grass, pasture

granarium, -ii (n.)—granary

grangia, -ie (f.)—grange; barn

granum, -i (n.)—grain

gratia, -e (f.)—favour, grace

grator (1, depon.)—to give thanks; to acknowledge

gratum, -i (n.)—goodwill, consent

    malo grato—against the will of

gratus, -a, -um (adj.)—acceptable, agreeable

grava, -e (f.)—a grove

gravamen, -inis (n.)—injury, grievance, oppression; accusation

gravis, -e (adj.)—heavy, severe, grievous

graviter (adv.)—heavily, severely

gressuma (see *gersuma*)

grossus, -a, -um (adj.)—thick, coarse

gula, -e (f.)—throat, gulley, watercourse

    g. Augusti, or *g. autumni*—Lammas-day

habeo, -ere, habui, habitum (2)—to have

habitus, -us (m.)—habit, dress

hactenus (adv.)—so far; so long, till now

haia, -e (f.)—hedge. Also *haya, -e* (f.); *hesea, -e* (f.)

harietum (see *herietum*)

harundo, -inis (f.)—reed

haya (see *haia*)

hayo (1)—to enclose with a hedge

hebdomada, -e (f.)—week; weekly routine or duty (eccles.)

heraldus, -i (m.)—herald

herbagium, -ii (n.)—pasture; right to pasture; payment for same

hercia, -e (f.)—a harrow

hercio (1)—to harrow

hereditamentum, -i (n.)—hereditament

hereditaria, -e (f.)—heiress

hereditarie (adv.)—by inheritance

hereditarius, -a, -um (adj.)—hereditary

hereditarius, -ii (m.)—heir

hereditatio, -ionis (f.)—inheritance

heredito (1)—to grant in fee or inheritance

heres, heredis (m., f.)—heir, heiress

herietum, -i (n.)—heriot. Also *harietum, -i* (n.)

heritagium, -ii (n.)—inheritance

hesea, -e (f.) (see *haia*)

hic, hec, hoc (pron. and adj.)—this

hida, -e (f.)—a hide of land

hidagium, -ii (n.)—hidage, tax

hiemalis, -e (adj.)—winter

hiems, hiemis (f.)—winter

hinc (adv.)—hence

 hinc inde—hereupon

hoga, -e (f.)—a how, mound

homagium, -ii (n.)—homage

homo, hominis (m.)—man

honestus, -a, -um (adj.)—honest, honourable; respectable

honor, -oris (m.)—honour, feudal honour, estate

honoranter (adv.)—honourably

honorifice (adv.)—honourably

hordeum (see *ordium*)

horreum, -ei (n.)—granary. Also *orreum*

hospitium, -ii (n.)—hospice, hospital, harbouring of someone

hospito (1)—to harbour

hostia, -ie (f.)—consecrated host (eccles.)

hostis, -is (m., gen.pl. *-ium*)—enemy

hucusque (adv.)—to this point; hitherto; till

Hugo, Hugonis (m.)—Hugo, Hugh

huiusmodi—of this kind, this kind of thing

humatus, -a, -um (adj.)—buried

humilis, -e (adj.)—lowly, humble

hundredum, -i (n.)—hundred (division of a county)

hutesium, -ii (n.)—hue-and-cry

hypodidasculus, -i (m.)—schoolmaster; usher

ibi (adv.)—there

ibidem (adv.)—at, or in, the same place

iconomus (for *oeconomus*)

idem, eadem, idem (pron.)—the same

ideo (adv.)—therefore

idoneus, -a, -um (adj.)—suitable

iens, euntis (pres. part. of *eo*)—going

ille, illa, illud (pron. and adj.)—that; he, she, it

illesus, -a, -um (past part.)—unharmed, inviolate

illuc (adv.)—thither

impechementum, -i (n.)—impediment

impechio (1)—to impeach

impediens, -ientis (m., f.; gen.pl. *-ium*)—defendant

impedimentum, -i (n.)—impediment, hindrance

impedio (4)—to hinder, to prevent

impendo, -ere, -di, -sum (3)—to lay out, expend

imperpetuum (adv.)—in perpetuity, forever

impetitio, -ionis (f.)—impeachment

impeto, -ere, -petivi, -petitum (3)—to impeach, to claim

implacito (1)—to plead, to implead. Also *implicito* (1)

impleo, -ere, -plevi, -pletum (2)—to fill; complete; fulfil, discharge

impono, -ere, -posui, -positum (3)—to lay upon; to impose; to impute, to charge with

imposterum (adv.)—hereafter, for the future

impotentia, -e (f.)—incapability

impressio, -ionis (f.)—stamp, impression

imprimis (adv.)—firstly, first

in (prep. with abl.)—in, into, on, at

in (prep. with acc.)—into, towards, within, to the limit of (of time); for, as (of purpose)

    in antea—beforehand, henceforth, for the future

    in manifesto—publicly

    in principali—in chief

    in prompto—promptly

    in proximo—soon

    in quantum—as far as

    in solidum—wholly, completely

    in vicem, or *invicem*—by turns, mutually, respectively. Also *in invicem*

incarnatio, -ionis (f.)—the Incarnation

incenso (1)—to cense

incipio, -ere, -cepi, -ceptum (3)—to begin

includo, -ere, -clusi, -clusum (3)—to enclose

incrementum, -i (n.)—land recently brought under cultivation

inculpamentum, -i (n.)—accusation, formal charge

inculpo (1)—to accuse, charge

incumbens, -entis (m.)—incumbent (eccles.)

incurro, -ere, -curri, -cursum (3)—to run into; to incur

inde (adv.)—thence, thereafter, then, in respect thereof, thereof, thereby, therefrom, therefor, thereupon

    hinc inde—hereupon

indebite, -arum (f.pl.)—dues

    i. fatigationis—dues for delaying eccles. lawsuit

indempnis, -e (adj.)—immune from injury or loss. Also *indempnus, -a, -um* (adj.)

indempnitas, -atis (f.)—indemnity

indentatus, -a, -um (past part.)—indented

indento (1)—to indent

indentura, -e (f.)—indenture

indicatio, -ionis (f.)—reward for giving information. Also *indicium, -ii* (n.)

induco, -ere, -duxi, -ductum (3)—to bring in; to induct

inductio, -ionis (f.)—induction

indulgentia, -e (f.)—indulgence

indulgeo, -ere, -dulsi, -dultum (2)—to grant an indulgence

indultum, -i (n.)—indulgence, grace

indultus, -us (m.)—leave, permission

inferius (adv.)—below; later

infero, -ferre, -tuli, -latum (3)—to bring into, to introduce, to inflict

infra (adv.)—below, overleaf, within

    infra breve—within a short time

infringo, -ere, -fregi, -fractum (3)—to break into, to violate, infringe

ingenuus, -ui (m.)—yeoman, freeholder

ingredior, -gredi, -gressus sum (3)—to enter, especially into property or rights

ingressus, -us (m.)—entry, right of entry into property or rights, dues paid for entry into possession

inhibeo (2)—to prevent, to restrain; to inhibit formally (eccles.)

inhibitio, -ionis (f.)—prohibition; inhibition (eccles.)

initiatus, -a (past part.)—baptized

iniungo, -ere, -iunxi, -iunctum (3)—to attach to; to impose, enjoin

iniuria, -e (f.)—wrong, injury, injustice

iniurio (1)—to wrong

iniuste (adv.)—unjustly

inquiro, -ere, -quisivi, -quisitum (3)—to search for, inquire into; to search for grounds for accusation

inquisitio, -ionis (f.)—inquiry, inquest

insero, -ere, -serui, -sertum (3)—to insert

insimul (adv.)—at the same time; together (of place or persons)

insisto, -ere, -stiti (3)—to apply oneself to

instancia, -ie (f.)—instance

instauratio, -ionis (f.)—stock

institutio, -ionis (f.)—institution to benefice (eccles.)

insulta, -e (f.)—assault, attack. Also *insultus, -us* (m.)

insulto (1)—to assault

insuper (adv. and prep.)—above, moreover, as mentioned above

integer, -gra, -grum (adj.)—whole, entire

integralis, -e (adj.)—whole, complete

integraliter (adv.)—wholly, in full

integre (adv.)—wholly, completely, in full

intellego, -ere, intellexi, intellectum (3)—to understand

intempto (1)—to accuse, charge

intencio, -ionis (f.)—meaning, purpose, intention. Also *intentio, -ionis* (f.); *intentus, -us* (m.)

inter (adv. and prep. with acc.)—between, betwixt, among

interdum (adv.)—sometimes

interea (adv.)—meanwhile

interesse (indeclinable)—interest (leg.)

interessentia, -e (f.)—interest on money

interest (impersonal verb with dat. of person)—it concerns, is of importance to

interficio, -ere, -feci, -fectum (3)—to destroy, to kill

interim (adv.)—meanwhile; for a while; sometimes

interpello (1)—to appeal, call upon

interrogo (1)—to interrogate

intersum, -esse, -fui—to be present at, attend

intestatus, -a, -um (adj.)—intestate. Also *ab intestato* (adv.)

intime (adv.)—deeply

intra (adv. and prep. with acc.)—within

intrare placitum—to enter a plea (leg.)

intro (1)—to enter; to bring in crops; to register

introitus, -us (m.)—entry, right of entry, appearance in court

intuitus, -us (m.)—look, view
intuitu—in respect of, in consideration of

intus (adv.)—within

invadio (1)—to pledge, mortgage

invenio, -ire, -veni, -ventum (4)—to come upon, find, furnish, provide

inventarium, -ii (n.)—list, inventory. Also *inventorium, -ii* (n.)

invicem (adv.) (*in vicem*; see *in*)

invirono (1)—to environ, surround

Iovis (see *die*)

ipse, ipsa, ipsum (pron. and adj.)—self, he himself, she herself, itself

irrotulatus, -a, -um (past part.)—enrolled

is, ea, id (pron. and adj.)—he, she, it; this, that

iste, ista, istud (pron. and adj.)—this

ita (adv.)—so, thus

item (adv.)—likewise, also, moreover

iter, itineris (n.)—journey; eyre, circuit of judges

itinerans, -antis (pres. part.)—travelling

itinero (1)—to travel

jacens, jacentis (pres. part.)—lying

jaceo, -ere, jacui, jacitum (2)—to lie, to be situate

jam (adv.)—now, at present, already, hitherto

jampna, -e (f.)—a heath. Also *janneta, -e* (f.); *jannum, -i* (n.)

jentaculum, -i (n.)—breakfast

Jovis (see *die*)

jubeo, -ere, jussi, jussum (2)—to order

judicium, -ii (n.)—judgement; statute; right; jurisdiction

jumentum, -i (n.)—mare

jungo, -ere, junxi, junctum (3)—to join

juramentum, -i (n.)—oath

jurator, -oris (m.)—juror

juro (1)—to swear
  juro ad, juro super—to swear on or by
  juro pro fidelitate—to swear fealty

jus, juris (n.)—law, right, due, privilege
  de iure—by rights, lawfully
  jure (adv.)—justly, lawfully

jussum, -i (n.)—command

juste (adv.)—justly

justiciarius, -ii (m.)—judge, justice

justifico (1)—to justify, set right; to bring to justice

justitia, -e (f.)—sentence; justice

justus, -a, -um (adj.)—lawful, just

juvenca, -e (f.)—heifer

juvenis, -e (adj.)—young

juxta (adv. and prep. with acc.)—near to, beside, according to
  juxta quod—according to

kidellus, -i (m.)—fish-trap

lagena, -e (f.)—a gallon

lana, -e (f.)—wool

lanatus, -a, -um (adj.)—clothed in wool (espec. for 'buried in wool')

lanceo (1)—to pierce, jut into, shoot into

largeo, -ere, -ui, -itum (2)—to bestow. Also *largio, -ire, -ivi, -itum* (4); *largior, -iri, -itus sum* (4, depon.)

largitas, -itatis (f.)—width

largitatio, -ionis (f.)—bestowal

largus, -a, -um (adj.)—wide
  ad largum—at large

latitudo, -inis (f.)—width, geographical latitude

latro, -onis (m.)—a thief

latum, -i (n.)—width

latus, -a, -um (adj.)—wide

laudabilis, -e (adj.)—praiseworthy

laudadiliter (adv.)—laudably

lavacrum, -i (n.)—font

lecternum, -i (n.)—lectern

lectus, -i (m.)—bed

legabilis, -e (adj.)—capable of being bequeathed

legalia, -ium (n.pl.)—laws, customs

legalis, -e (adj.)—law-worthy, of legal status, loyal; lawful

legantia, -e (f.)—legacy. Also *legatio, -ionis* (f.)

legatinus, -a, -um (adj.)—of or for a papal legate

legatorius, -ii (m.; *-ia* (f.))—legatee. Also *legatarius, -ii*

legitime (adv.)—lawfully

legitimus, -a, -um (adj.)—law-worthy, of legal status; having complete powers of disposition (leg.)

legius (see *ligius*)

lego (1)—to depute, appoint as deputy, to bequeath as a legacy, to leave

lego, -ere, -legi, -lectum (3)—to read

lenocinium, -ii (n.)—pandering; enticement

leta, -e (f.)—leet

leucata, -e (f.)—measure of land, league. Also *leuuga*

levatio, -ionis (f.)—raising, lifting
l. *feni*—hay-making

levo (1)—to raise; to levy dues

lex, legis (f.)—law

liber, libera, liberum (adj.)—free

liberalis, -e (adj.)—free, free-born

liberaliter (adv.)—freely, without compulsion

liberatio, -ionis (f.)—delivery, handing over, payment

liberator, -oris (m.)—feoffor

libere (adv.)—freely

liberi, -orum (pl.m.)—children

libero (1)—to hand over; to warrant; to pay (money). Also *libro* (1)

libertas, -tatis (f.)—privileged area, franchise, liberty. Also *livertas, -tatis* (f.)

libra, -e (f.)—pound

libro (see *libero*)

liceat (pres. subjunct.)—let it be lawful or allowed

licentia, -e (f.)—permission, authorization

licentio (1)—to permit, authorize, give leave to depart, dismiss

licet (impersonal verb)—it is allowed, it is lawful

licet (used as a conjunction)—even if, although, granted that

licite (adv.)—lawfully

ligius, -a, -um (adj.)—liege; independent, having complete powers of disposition (leg.). Also *legius*

lignagium, -ii (n.)—timber; right to take timber
lignarium, -ii (n.)—timber; right to take timber; also timberyard

lignum, -i (n.)—wood; beam

ligo (1)—to bind

limes, -itis (m.)—cross-path; balk; boundary

linea, -ee (f.)—sheet for wearing while doing penance

linum, -i (n.)—flax; linen

liquet (impersonal verb)—it is clear, it appears; *liquit* (past tense)

liquidus, -a, -um (adj.)—clear

lis, litis (f., gen.pl. -ium)—dispute; accusation; law-suit

litera, -e (f.)—letter; charter, deed. Also *littera, -e* (f.)

literatura, -e (f.)—learning

litigiosus, -a, -um (adj.)—subject to dispute

livertas (see *libertas*)

locacio, -ionis (f.)—a placing, locating, hire, wages. Also *locatio*

loco (1)—to take on lease, to hire; to lease, to farm out, to place

locus, -i (m.)—a place

loga, -e (f.)—lodge, hut. Also *logia, -e* (f.)

longitudo, -inis (f.)—length, geographical longitude

longus, -a, -um (adj.)—long
a longe—round about, indirectly
in longum—in length

loquela, -e (f.)—suit, action

loquelor (1, depon.)—to plead, implead; to confer on a point (leg.)

lucrabilis, -e (adj.)—profitable; arable

lucro (1)—to make a profit on; to gain

lucrum, -i (n.)—interest on money

Lune (see *die*)

magis (adv.)—more

magister, magistri (m.)—master; title of cleric with Master's degree

magnopere (adv.)—greatly

magnus, -a, -um (adj.)—great, large, senior, the elder

maior, maius (adj.; Kennedy, p. 25, §51)—greater

major, majoris (adj.)—of age

major, majoris (m.)—mayor, magnate

male (adv.)—badly

malus, -a, -um (adj.)—bad

mandatorius, -ii (m.)—apparitor of eccles. court

mando (1)—to commission, command, enjoin

mane (n., indeclinable)—morning; in the morning

maneo, -ere, mansi, mansum (2)—to remain, stay, dwell

manerialis, -e (adj.)—of or for a manor

manerium, -ii (n.)—manor

manifestim (adj.)—manifestly

manifestus, -a, -um (adj.)—evident, manifest

in manifesto (see *in*)

manimola (see *manumolendinum*)

mano (1)—to flow; to issue

mansum, -i (n.)—dwelling-house

manucapio, -ere, -cepi, -captum (3)—to undertake, to go bail for

manucaptio, -ionis (f.)—bail, mainprise

manucaptor, -oris (m.)—surety, mainpernor

manumolendinum, -i (n.)—handmill. Also *manimola, -e* (f.)

manus, -us (f.)—hand

manus mortua (f.)—mortmain

manutenementum, -i (n.)—maintenance, support. Also *manutenentia, -e* (f.)

manuteneo, -ere, -tenui, -tentum (2)—to maintain, support

manutergium, -ii (n.)—towel

mappa, -e (f.)—map; cloth

marca, -e (f.)—a mark. Also *mercata, -e* (f.)

mare, -is (n.; decl. Kennedy, p. 16, §31)—sea

maresium, -ii (n.)—marsh. Also *mariscus, -i* (m.); *meresium, -ii* (n.)

maritagium, -ii (n.)—marriage-portion, dowry. Also *mariagium*

maritatio, -ionis (f.)—marriage, giving in marriage, right of marriage

marito (1)—to marry

marlaria, -ie (f.)—marl-pit. Also *marlera*

marlo (1)—to marl land

Martis (see *die*)

Martius, -ii (m.)—March (*mensis* understood)

masagium (see *messuagium*)

masculus, -i (adj. and noun)—masculine, male

masura, -e (f.) (see *messuagium*)

mater, matris (f.)—mother

materia, -e (f.)—material, timber

matertera, -e (f.)—an aunt, mother's sister

Matildis, -em, -is, -i, -e (f.)—Matilda

matutine, -arum (f.pl.)—matins

maxime (adv.)—especially

maximus, -a, -um (adj.)—greatest

medietas, -atis (f.)—moiety, half

mel, mellis (n.)—honey

melior, melius (adj., decl. Kennedy, p. 24, §49)—better

melius (adv.)—better

membrum, -i (n.)—limb, member, part, portion

memoro (1)—to mention

mensa, -e (f.)—table

mensis, -is (m.)—month

mentiono (1)—to mention. Also *menciono* (1)

mercata (see *marca*)

mercator, -oris (m.)—merchant

Mercurii (see *die*)

meremium, -ii (n.)—timber

meresium (see *maresium*)

meridies, -iei (m.)—noon; the south

messarius, -ii (m.)—hayward. Also *messerarius; messor, -oris*

messerium, -ii (n.)—mowing, reaping, harvest. Also *messurcium, -ii* (n.); *mestiva, -e* (f.)

messuagium, -ii (n.)—messuage, house, holding. Also *mesuagium; masagium; masura*

meta, -e (f.)—boundary-stone, boundary

meto, -ere, messui, messum (3)—to reap

Michaelis, -is (m.)—Michael; Michaelmas

miles, militis (m.)—knight

militaris, -e (adj.)—of, or for, a knight

mille—a thousand

millesimus, -a, -um (adj.)—one thousandth

minime (adv.)—least

minimus, -a, -um (adj.)—least, smallest

minister, -tri (m.)—minor official, reeve, bailiff, sergeant; minister (eccles.)

ministro (1)—to serve as minister or priest; to administer (sacraments)

minor, minus (adj.; Kennedy, p. 25, §51)—lesser, smaller

minus (adv.)—less

misa, -orum (n.pl.)—outlay, expense; agreement

miseracio, -ionis (f.)—mercy; amercement

misericordia, -e (f.)—mercy, amercement

missa, -e (f.)—Mass

mitto, -ere, misi, missum (3)—to send; to place; to lay a pledge, to contribute

mixtilio, -ionis (f.)—maslin

modius, -ii (m.)—a liquid measure

modo (adv.)—only; now, lately

modus, -i (m.)—measure, manner, method

modus (*decimandi*)—modus, payment in lieu of tithe in kind

molendarius, -ii (m.)—a miller. Also *molendinarius*

molendinum, -i (n.)—mill

monacha, -e (f.)—nun

monachalis, -e (adj.)—of or for a monk, monastic

monachus, -i (m.)—monk

moneo (2)—to warn; to summon

moneta, -e (f.)—coined money, money

mora, -e (f.)—moor, marsh.

moram trahere (see *traho*)

mores, -um (m.pl.)—character

morior, mori, mortuus sum (3, depon.)—to die

moror (1, depon.)—to delay, remain, dwell

mors, mortis (f.)—death

mortuarium, -ii (n.)—mortuary payment

mortuarius, -a, -um (adj.)—of or for a mortuary payment

mortuus, -a, -um (adj., past part.)—dead

mos, moris (m.)—custom

moveo, -ere, movi, motum (2)—to move, stir up, provoke

mulier, -ieris (f.)—woman; wife

multimode (adv.)—in many ways

multum (adv.)—much

multus, -a, -um (adj.)—many

munimen, -inis (n.)—strengthening, fortification, confirmation

murilegus, -i (m.)—a cat

muto (1)—to change, exchange, lend

mutuum, -ui (n.)—a loan

ex mutuo—on loan

namium,—ii (n.)—distraint, goods distrained

natale, -is (n., gen.pl. *-ium*)—birth, birthday

natalis, -e (adj.)—belonging to one's birth

nativitas, -itatis (f.)—birth

nativus, -a, -um (adj.)—born, native

terra nativa—land held by villein tenure

nativus, -i (m.)—villein, serf

naturalis, -e (adj.)—natural

natus, -a, -um (past part.)—born

nec (conj.)—and not, nor. Also *neque*

nec . . . nec—neither . . . nor. Also *neque . . . neque*

necessarius, -a, -um (adj.)—needful, necessary

necessitas, -atis (f.)—necessity; relationship, connection

necne (adv.)—or not; sometimes used for *necnon*

necnon—and also, and in fact, and yet

negative (adv.)—negatively

nego (1)—to deny

negotium, -ii (n.)—business

nemo, neminis (m., f.)—no one

nemorosus, -a, -um (adj.)—wooded

nemus, nemoris (n.)—a wood

neque (see *nec*)

nescio, -ire, -scivi, -scitum (4)—not to know, be ignorant

nichil (see *nihil*)

Nicholaus, -ai (declines like *dominus*)— Nicholas

nihil (indeclin. n.)—nothing. Also *nichil*

nihilominus (adv.)—nonetheless

nimis (adv.)—too much, excessively

nisi (conj.)—if not, unless; except

nocumentum, -i (n.)—harm, damage, nuisance, harmful thing

nolo, nolle, nolui (irreg.)—to be unwilling, not to wish

nomen, nominis (n.)—name; title

  nomine (with genitive)—in the name of; in respect of; under the heading of

nominatim (adv.)—by name

nominatus, -a, -um (past part.)— named

nomino (1)—to name

non (adv.)—not

nonagesimus, -a, -um (adj.)—ninetieth

nonaginta (indeclin.)—ninety

nonconformis, -is, (m., f.)—nonconformist

nondum (adv.)—not yet

nongenti, -e, -a—nine hundred

nonsolutio, -ionis (f.)—non-payment

nonus, -a, -um (adj.)—ninth

nos, nostrum (pron.)—we

nosco, -ere, novi, notum (3)—to get to know; past tenses have the meaning 'to know'

noster, -tra, -trum (adj.)—our

nothus, -i (m.)—bastard

notitia, -e (f.)—knowledge, cognizance

notorius, -ii (m.)—notary

notus, -a, -um (past part.)—known

novem—nine

novus, -a, -um (adj.)—new

  de novo—anew

nox, noctis (f.)—night

numero (1)—to count, reckon, number

nunc (adv.)—now

nuncupo (1)—to call by name, to name

nundinatio, -ionis (f.)—market

nuntiatus, -ii (m.)—messenger (often *apparitor* in eccles. court)

nuntius, -ii (m.)—messenger

nuper (adv.)—lately, recently

nuper (used as an adj.)—the late

nuptialis, -e (adj.)—nuptial, pertaining to a wedding

nuptie, -iarum (f.pl.)—marriage, nuptials. Also *nupcie, -iarum* (f.pl.)

obediens, -ientis (adj.)—obedient

obedientia, -e (f.)—jurisdiction, homage, oath of homage; monastic office, revenues of same; monastic vow of obedience

obedio, -ire, -ii, or *-ivi, -itum* (4)—to obey

obeo, -ire, -ii, obitum (4)—to die

obicio, -ere, -ieci, -iectum (3)—to oppose, to object

obitus, -us (m.)—death; anniversary service for dead, obit

objectio, -ionis (f.)—formal charge in eccles. court. Also *objectum, -i* (n.)

objecto (1)—to charge in eccles. court

oblatio, -ionis (f.)—offering; payment

oblegantia, -e (f.)—bond. Also *obliga-men, -inis* (n.); *obligatorium, -ii* (n.)

obligo (1)—to bind

obolus, -i (m.)—half-penny

obsequia, -orum (n.pl.)—obsequies

obsequium, -ii (n.)—divine service

obsisto, -ere, -stiti, -stitum (3)—to oppose, obstruct

obstipuo (1)—to stop up. Also *obstupuo*

obsto, -are, -stiti, -statum (1)—to withstand, obstruct

obstruo, -ere, -struxi, -structum (3)—to obstruct

obtineo (see *optineo*)

obvencio, -ionis (f.)—income, revenue; offering, obvention

occidens, -entis (m.)—the west

occidentalis, -e (adj.)—western

occido, -ere, -cidi, -cisum (3)—to kill

occupator, -oris (m.)—occupier, possessor, usurper

occupatum, -i (n.)—purpresture, land unlawfully occupied

occupo (1)—to seize, occupy

octaba, -e (f., and in pl.)—an octave, eighth day inclusive; eight days inclusive. Also *octava, -e* (and in pl.)

octavus, -a, -um (adj.)—eighth

octingenti, -e, -a—eight hundred

octo (indeclin.)—eight

octoginta (indeclin.)—eighty

oeconomus, -i (m.)—steward; churchwarden

offero, -erre, obtuli, oblatum (3)—to offer; bring, bestow

officialis, -is (m.)—officer, 'official' of bishop or archdeacon

officina, -e (f.)—outbuilding, domestic office

officium, -ii (n.)—divine service, trade, calling, office, workshop, outbuilding

   o. merum—the 'mere' office of an eccles. judge

o. promotum—the proceedings of an eccles. judge 'promoted' by information given

oleum, -ei (n.)—oil

olla, -e (f.)—pot, jar

omnimode, omnimodum (adv.)—in every way, entirely

omnimodus, -a, -um (adj.)—of every kind

omnino (adv.)—in every way, entirely

omnis, -e (adj.)—all, every

onero (1)—to load, to charge, to make answerable for, debit with; to surcharge, i.e. to pasture more animals than allowed

onus, -eris (n.)—burden, load; force, effect; charge (in accounts)

operatio, -ionis (f.)—operation, effect, performing of work or services due, daywork

operator, -oris (m.)—workman

opero (1)—to perform work or services due

opportunus, -a, -um (adj.)—seasonable

oppositum, -i (n.)—an opposing, a citing against

optime (adv.)—best

optimus, -a, -um (adj.)—best

optineo, -ere, -tinui, -tentum (2)—to obtain, maintain, possess

opus, operis (n.)—work, customary service, maintenance, daywork, use

opus est mihi—I have need of

ordinabiliter (adv.)—in due form

ordinacio, -ionis (f.)—regulation, ordinance; ordination (eccles.)

ordinarius, -ii (m.)—one having 'Ordinary' jurisdiction

ordinator, -oris (m.)—ordainer

ordino (1)—to appoint; arrange

ordium, -ii (n.)—barley. Also *ordeum; hordeum*

ordo, -inis (m.)—order (eccles.)

organizo (1)—to play the organ

oriens, -tis (m.)—the east

orientalis, -e (adj.)—eastern

originale, -is (n.)—original document

originalis, -e (adj.)—original

oriundus, -a, -um (adj.)—descended, sprung, born, originating in or from

orreum (see *horreum*)

ostendo, -ere, -di, -sum (3)—to show

otiosus, -a, -um (adj.)—unemployed, esp. of animals not used for ploughing

oviale, -is; also *ovile, -is* (both n., gen.pl. *-ium*)—sheepfold

ovis, -is (f., gen.pl. *-ium*)—sheep

pacatus, -a, -um (past part.)—pacified, quiet, satisfied, paid

pacifico (1)—to appease, pacify

pacificus, -a, -um (adj.)—peaceable

padnagium (see *pannagium*)

pagina, -e (f.)—page, deed, document

palma, -e (f.)—palm. Plural is used for Palm Sunday. Also, *dies palmarum*—Palm Sunday

panellus, -i (m.)—panel; sheet; list

panis, -is (m.)—loaf, bread

pannagio (1)—to pasture pigs

pannagium, -ii (n.)—pannage, right of pannage, dues paid for same

pannus, -i (m.)—cloth

papa, -e (m.)—the Pope

papalis, -e (adj.)—papal

papistria, -e (f.)—papistry

par, paris (adj.)—equal

par, paris (n., decl. Kennedy, p. 16, §31)—a pair

paraphernalia (n.pl., gen. *-ium*)—the property of a married woman

Parasceve, -is (n.)—Good Friday. Also *dies parascevensis*

parca, -e (f.)—park, pound, enclosure. Also *parcus, -i* (m.); *parrocus, -i* (m.)

parcagium, -ii (n.)—dues for repairing fences

parcata (see *pertica*)

parcella, -e (f.)—part, portion, parcel, detail, item. Also *percella*

parcenarius, -ii (m.)—parcener, joint-owner

parco (1)—to enclose; to impound

parens, -tis (m. and f.)—parent, grandparent, ancestor

parentela, -e (f.)—family, kindred, relationship

paria, -ie (f.)—a pair

paries, -etis (m.)—wall

parifico (1)—to make equal

pariformiter (adv.)—in like manner, equally

pariter (adv.)—equally

parochia, -e (f.)—parish

parochialia (n.pl., gen. *-ium*)—dues paid to clergy of a parish

parochialis, -e (adj.)—parochial

parochianus, -i (m.)—member of a diocese, parishioner

parochius, -ii (m.)—parish priest

parrocus (see *parca*)

pars, partis (f., gen.pl. *-ium*)—part; party (leg.)

  p. actrix, -icis (f.)—plaintiff(s)

  p. defendens, -entis (f.)—defendant(s)

  p. rea (f.)—defendant(s)

  ex parte—on behalf of

  in hac parte—in this matter or business

  per partem—by means of

partes, -ium (f.pl.)—district, region

parsona (see *persona*)

partica (see *pertica*)

participatio, -ionis (f.)—a sharing

particula, -e (f.)—detail, item

particulariter (adv.)—separately, one by one, in detail

partitio, -ionis (f.)—separation (in marriage)

parvus, -a, -um (adj.)—small

Pascha, -e (f.)—Easter Sunday. Also *Pascha, Paschatis* (n.)

Pascha floridum—Palm Sunday

paschalis, -e (adj.)—of or for Easter *dies paschalis*—Easter Sunday

pasco, pascere, pavi, pastum (3)—to feed, to pasture

pascor, pasci, pastus sum (3, depon.)—to feed, to graze

pascua, -e (f.)—pasture

pascualis, -e (adj.)—of or for pasture

pascuum, -i (n.)—service of providing pasture

passagium, -ii (n.)—passage; right of passage-way

Passio, -ionis (f.)—the Passion, Passion Week

pastura, -e (f.)—pasture, right of pasture

pasturo (1)—to graze

pateat (see *pateo*)

patena, -e (f.)—paten

patens, -entis (adj.)—open, patent *littere patentes* (f.pl.)—letters patent *patens, -entis* (f. gen.pl. *-ium*)—a letter patent

pateo, -ere, patui (2)—to be open, to be clear or manifest *pateat* (pres. subj.)—let it be known, manifest

pater, -ris (m.)—father

paternitas, -tatis (f.)—fatherhood (as title, eccles.)

patria, -e (f.)—county, district, neighbourhood, inhabitants of a district, jury

patronatus, -us (m.)—advowson

patronus, -i (m.)—patron of a benefice

paullum, paulum, paulo (adv.)—a little, somewhat

pauper, -eris (adj., decl. Kennedy, p. 23)—poor

paupertas, -atis (f.)—poverty

pavagium, -ii (n.)—pavage, toll

pax, pacis (f.)—peace, consent, agreement

pecia, -ie (f.)—piece, portion. Also *peciata, -e* (f.); *pecies, -iei* (f.)

pecunia, -ie (f.)—cattle; cash *pecunia viva*—livestock

peior, peius (adj.)—worse. Also *pejor.* *peius* (adv.)—worse

pejoratio, -ionis (f.)—injury, deterioration

pejoro (1)—to injure. Also *pegoro*

pellis, -is (f.)—a skin, hide

pena, -e (f.)—penalty, punishment, pain, compensation

pendeo, -ere, pependi (2)—to hang, be suspended

pendo, -ere, pependi, pensum (3)—to weigh

pene (adv.)—nearly, almost

penes (prep. with accus.)—in possession or power of; towards; as regards

penitens, -entis (m, f.)—a penitent

penitentia, -e (f.)—penance (eccles.)

penitentio (1)—to do penance

penitus (adv.)—inwardly, from within, wholly

penosa (see *Septimana penosa*)

pensionarius, -a, -um (adj.)—paying or receiving a pension

per (prep. with accus.)—through, by, by means of, throughout, during or in the course of, on pain of; at, on, in, about (of time and place), on payment of *per ante, per antea*—before, formerly *per austrum*—southwards *per consequens*—in consequence *per extra*—outside *per omnia*—in all respects *per sic quod*—on condition that, to the effect that *per transversum*—across *per vicem*—at times, occasionally *perambulatio, -ionis* (f.)—walking the bounds of a parish

percella (see *parcella*)

percha (see *pertica*)

percipio, -ere, -cepi, -ceptum (3)—to seize, occupy; to understand, perceive

percutio, -ere, -cussi, -cussum (3)—to strike

perditio, -ionis (f.)—loss, injury

perditus, -a, -um (past part.)—lost, ruined

perdo, -ere, perdidi, perditum (3)—to ruin, waste, lose

perdono (1)—to give, grant

pergamenum, -i (n.)—parchment

pergravo (1)—to oppress

periculum, -i (n.)—peril

perimpleo, -ere, -plevi, -pletum (3)—to fill up completely, to carry out completely

perinde (adv.)—in the same manner, just as, equally; by or through that place

permaneo, -ere, -mansi, -mansum (2)—to last, to remain, endure

permissio, -ionis (f.)—permission

peroptime (adv.)—thoroughly, very well

perpaco (1)—to pay in full

perpetualis, -e (adj.)—continual, everlasting

perpetualiter (adv.)—perpetually, forever. Also *perpetue* (adv.)

perpetuum, -i (n.)—lifetime

perpetuus, -a, -um (adj.)—continual, everlasting, perpetual

perporto (see *proporto*)

perquero (see *perquiro*)

perquiro, -ere, -quisivi, -quisitum (3)—to seek for; to restore; to obtain, acquire, purchase

perquiro cum—to purchase of or from

perquisitio, -ionis (f.)—gain, profit, perquisite, purchase

perquisitum, -i (n.)—thing acquired

perquisitum curie—profits from the manorial court

perquisitor, -oris (m.)—purchaser

persolutio, -ionis (f.)—repeated payment, perquisite, compensation, payment in full

persona, -e (m.)—parson; parsonage, rectory. Also *parsona*

personaliter (adv.)—in person

personatus, -us (m.)—an eccles. benefice; parsonage

persono (1)—to institute to a benefice

pertica, -e (f.)—measure of length or of land, perch. Also *perticata; partica; parcata; percha*

pertinens, -entis (pres. part.)—pertaining

pertinentia, -e (f.)—appurtenance

pertineo, -ere, -tinui (2)—to belong to, pertain to

perturbatrix, -icis (f.)—a disturber (female)

pervenio, -ire, -veni, -ventum (4)—to arrive at, reach a place; to come to, to fall to (of inheritance, etc.)

pessime (adv.)—most badly

pessimus, -a, -um (adj.)—worst

pestrinum (see *pistorium*)

petens, -entis (m., f., gen.pl. *-ium*)—plaintiff

peto, -ere, petivi (or *-ii*), *-itum* (3)—to require, seek, claim, petition

petra, -e (f.)—stone (building material); a stone (weight); gravestone

petrinum (see *pistorium*)

pietas, pietatis (f.)—dutifulness, piety

pileus, -e (m.)—a felt cap. Also *pilius*

pinguis, -e (adj.)—fat

piper, -eris (n.)—pepper

piper rotundus (m., collective noun)—peppercorns

piscaria, -e (f.)—fishing, right to fish

piscis, -is (m.)—fish

pistor, -oris (m.)—miller, baker

pistorium, -ii (n.)—bakery, bakehouse. Also *pistura, -e* (f.); *pistrinum, -i* (n.); *pestrinum, petrinum, pistrinum*

pisum, -i (n.)—a pea, peas

placea, -e (f.)—open space, piece of ground, place, residence. Also *placia, -e* (f.); *plecia*

placea nundinationis—market-place

placeo, -ere, -ui, -itum (2)—to please (with object in dative)

placito (1)—to plead

placitum, -i (n.)—plea

intrare placitum (see *intrare*)

plana, -e (f.)—field as opposed to wood

planus, -a, -um (adj.)—level or open

de plano—summarily

plaustrum, -i (n.)—wagon, cart

plebanus, -i (m.)—rural dean

plebeius, -ei (m.)—layman

plegagium, -ii (n.)—pledge, security

p. liberum—frankpledge

plegius, -ii (m.)—one who goes bail, surety; bail, security; pledge

plenarie (adv.)—fully

plenarius, -ia, -ium (adj.)—full, complete

plene (adv.)—fully

plenitudo, -inis (f.)—fulness; plenarty (condition of eccles. benefice when occupied)

plenius (adv.)—more fully

plenus, -a, -um (adj.)—full

plevina, -e (f.)—pledge, security

plumbum, -i (n.)—lead

pluralitas, -atis (f.)—plurality

plurimum (adv.)—mostly

plurimus, -a, -um (adj.)—most

plus, pluris (adj., Kennedy, p. 25, §51) —more

plus (adv.)—more

poderis, -is (m.)—an alb

pomarium, -ii (n.)—orchard. Also *pomerium*

pondero (1)—to weigh (as 'to weigh a lb.')

pondus, -eris (n.)—weight

pone (adv. and prep.)—behind, beside

pono, -ere, posui, positum (3)—to place, appoint, produce in court (leg.)

p. ad—to put to, set to

p. in defenso—to put in defence, forbid entry to

p. in respectum—to adjourn, respite

p. se in—to put oneself on, submit to (leg.)

populus, -i (m.)—people

porcaria, -e (f.)—pigsty, piggery. Also *porcheria*

porcarius, -ii (m.)—swineherd

porcellus, -i (m.)—piglet

porcinus, -a, -um (adj.)—of a pig

porcina, -e (f.)—pork

porcus, -i (m.)—a pig

porta, -e (f.)—gate

portio, -ionis (f.)—share, part, portion; part of a benefice which is divided. Also *porcio*

porto (1)—to bear, carry

p. breve—to take out a writ

positio, -ionis (f.)—a placing, position; statement, charge (leg.)

posse (see *possum*)

posse (indeclin., n.)—power, force, ability

pro posse—as far as possible

posse comitatus—effective force of a county

possessio, -ionis (f.)—possession, occupation, property

possessionator, -oris (m.)—possessor. Also *possessionatus, -i* (m.)

possessionor (1, deponent)—to own, be possessed of

possideo, -ere, -sedi, -sessum (2)—to own, possess, occupy

possum, posse, potui—to be able

post (adv. and prep. with acc.)—behind, after, afterwards, according to

postdisseisina, -e (f.)—post-disseisin

postea (adv.)—hereafter, thereafter, afterwards

posteritas, -itatis (f.)—posterity

posterum (adv.)—later, afterwards. Also *in posterum*

in posteris—for the future, hereafter

posthac (adv.)—hereafter, henceforth

postmodo, or *postmodum* (adv.)—afterwards

postquam (conj.)—after

potestas, -tatis (f.)—power, dominion, area of jurisdiction

potestas ligia—complete power of disposition (leg.)

potestativus, -a, -um (adj.)—subject to will (leg.)

potior, -iri, potitus sum (4, depon., with object in ablative)—to obtain, get possession of

prae (see *pre*)

prandium, -ii (n.)—dinner

prata, -e (f.)—meadow

praticulum, -i (n.)—small meadow

pratum, -i (n.)—meadow, meadow-land

pre (adv. and prep. with abl.)—before

pre (for *per*)—through, over

pre ante—before

pre manibus—beforehand, in advance

prebenda, -e (m.)—prebend

prebendarius, -a, -um (adj.)—prebendary

prebendarius, -ii (m.)—provender; prebendary. Also *prebendatus, -us* (m.)

prebeo (2)—to offer; to render, give; to show

precaria, -e (f.)—boon-work. Also *precarium, -ii* (n.)

precarius, -ii (m.)—a boon-worker

dies precarius—boonday

precedens, -entis (adj.)—preceding

precipe, p. in capite, p. quod reddat—the name of a writ (leg.)

precipio, -ere, -cepi, -ceptum (3)—to take or receive beforehand, to get or receive in advance; to advise, teach, order

precipue (adv.)—principally, especially

precise (adv.)—exactly, precisely

preconcedo, -ere, -cessi, -cessum (3)—to grant previously or beforehand

preconcessa, -orum (n.pl.)—things granted previously

preconizatio, -ionis (f.)—public calling in eccles. court

precontractus, -us (m.)—precontract of marriage. Also *preconventio, -ionis* (f.)

predecessor, -oris (m.)—predecessor, ancestor, forebear

predico, -ere, -dixi, -dictum (3)—to say beforehand

predictus, -a, -um (past part.)—aforesaid

predilectus, -a, -um (adj.)—well-beloved

preexcipio, -ere, -cepi, ceptum (3)—to except beforehand

preexigo, -ere, -exegi, -exactum (3)—to require beforehand

prefatus, -a, -um (adj.)—aforesaid

prefectura, -e (f.)—office of reeve

prefectus, -i (m.)—reeve

prefero, -ferre, -tuli, -latum (3)—to prefer to an eccles. benefice

prefor, -fari, -fatus sum (1, depon.)—to say beforehand

prelatus, -i (m.)—official, reeve, feudal lord; prelate (eccles.)

premissa, -orum (n.pl.)—premisses, things mentioned before

premunio, -ire, -ivi, -itum (4)—to warn, give notice of, cite, summon

premunire—(15th cent.) the name of a writ (leg.); (16th cent.) offence against the statute of *premunire*

premunitio, -ionis (f.)—warning, notice

prenomino (1)—to mention or name before

prenoto (1)—to mention before

prepositura, -e (f.)—office of reeve; office of provost

prepositus, -i (m.)—prior, abbot; reeve
p. regis—royal official

prerecito (1)—to mention beforehand

prerogo (1)—to grant, give

presbyter, -eri (m.)—priest

presbyteratus, -us (m.)—office of priest; priesthood

prescribo, -ere, -scripsi, -scriptum (3)— to prescribe, to claim by lapse of time (leg.)

prescriptio, -ionis (f.)—right created by lapse of time

presens, -entis (adj.)—present

presentes, -ium (f.pl.)—'presents', 'these presents', i.e. letters, document, deed

presentatio, -ionis (f.)—presentment (leg.); right of presentation to an ecclesiastical benefice

presentatus, -i (m.)—presentee (to eccles. benefice)

presentia, -e (f.)—present, gift. Also *presentum, -i* (n.)

presentialiter (adv.)—in person

presento (1)—to give, to show; to present to an eccles. benefice; to make a presentment

presolvo, -ere, -solvi, -solutum (3)—to pay beforehand; especially *presolutus, -a, -um* (past part.)—paid beforehand

prestaria, -e (f.)—grant of lease

prestarius, -ii (m.)—borrower

prestitum (n.)—loan or payment of money

presto (1)—to lend; to take an oath

preter (adv. and prep. with acc.)— past, beyond, except, besides

preterea (adv.)—besides, moreover; henceforth

preteritus, -a, -um (past part.)—past

pretium, -ii (n.)—price, value

prex, precis (f.)—prayer

primitus (adv.)—in the first place

primus, -a, -um (adj.)—first

principalis, -e (adj.)—in chief (of feudal lords or tenants); chief
in p. (see *in*)

prior, prius (adj., decl. Kennedy, p. 24, §49)—former, first

prior, -oris (m.)—prior (eccles.)

pristinus, -a, -um (adj.)—former, original, pristine

prius (adv.) (see also *prior*)—before, first, previously

pro (prep. with abl.)—for; during; in; as far as; in accordance with; in return for
pro certo—certainly
pro expensis—at the expense of
pro forma—according to form
pro libito—at will
pro nunc—at or for the present
pro parte—on behalf of
pro partibus—in proportion
pro perpetuito—forever
pro placito—at will, at pleasure
pro posse—as far as possible
pro tunc—then, at that time
pro velle—at will, at pleasure

proavus, -i (m.)—great-grandfather; forefather

probacio, -ionis (f.)—probate of will

probo (1)—to approve; to prove (esp. wills)

probus, -a, -um (adj.)—upright, good
homo probus—good man (leg.)

procedo, -ere, -cessi, -cessum (3)—to proceed

processus, -us (m.)—legal process, proceedings

procreatus, -a, -um (past part.)—begotten

procreo (1)—to beget

procurator, -oris (m.)—monastic official; proctor

produco, -ere, -duxi, -ductum (3)—to bring forward, to produce

p. sectam—to bring suit, bring evidence (leg.)

professor,-oris (m.)—doctor (academic)

proficuum, -ui (n.)—profit. Also *proficium, -ii* (n.); *perficium,* -ii (n.)

prohibeo, -ere, -ui, -itum (2)—to forbid

proles, -is (f.)—offspring, descendant

promotor, -oris (m.)—mover of office of judge in eccles. cause

promoveo, -ere, -movi, -motum (2)—to promote

prompto or *in prompto* (adv.)—promptly

promptuarium, -ii (n.)—store-room

promptus, -a, -um (adj.)—ready (of money)

propars (see *purpars*)

propinquarius, -ii (m.)—kinsman, relation

propinquior, -ioris (adj. and noun)—nearer, nearest, next; having the first claim or right, nearest relation

propinquuus,-a,-um (adj.)—near, neighbouring

proporto (1)—to purport, state, show. Also *perporto; purporto*

se proporto—to appear, be manifest

propositum, -i (n.)—plan, purpose

proprietas, -tatis (f.)—property, owning of property (eccles.)

proprius, -a, -um (adj.)—one's own, special, proper

propter (adv. and prep. with acc.)—near, close to, on account of, because of

propterea (adv.)—therefore

prosequor, -sequi, -secutus sum (3, depon.)—to prosecute, pursue, follow out

prosterno, -ere, -stravi, -stratum (3)—to level, fill up; to fell

prout (adv.)—according as, in proportion, just as, proportionably as

provenio, -ire, -veni, -ventum (4)—to come forth; to issue; to result from (of revenue or profits)

proventus, -us (m.)—income, proceeds

proviso quod (with subj.)—provided that. Also *proviso ut*

proxime (adv.)—nearest, next, lastly. Also *proximo* (*in proximo,* see *in*)

proximus, -a, -um (adj.)—the nearest, next

pudor, -oris (m.)—shame, affront, dishonour

puella, -e (f.)—girl

puer, -eri (m.)—boy

pulla, -e (f.)—chicken; filly

pullus, -i (m.)—chicken; colt

pulpitum, -i (n.)—pulpit

pure (adv.)—purely, unconditionally ·

purgacio, -ionis (f.)—clearing by compurgation or ordeal (leg.)

puro (1)—to grant in pure almoign; to liquidate debts

purpars, -partis (f., gen.pl. *-ium*)—purparty, share. Also *purpartia, -e* (f.); *propars*

purprestura, -e (f.)—purpresture, encroachment

purus, -a, -um (adj.)—pure, absolute, unconditional, clear; net (of accounts)

puto (1)—to think, to suppose

Quadragesima, -e (f.)—Lent

quadragesimalis, -e (adj.)—Lenten

quadraginta—forty

quadrans, quadrantis (m.)—farthing

quadringenti, -e, -a (pl.)—four hundred

qualis, -e (adj. and pron.)—of what kind, what kind of a; of such a kind, such as *qualiter* (adv.)—in what way or manner, how; by what right; (with subj.) in such a way that

qualitercumque (adv.)—in what way soever, howsoever, soever

quam (adv.)—in what manner, how, how much, as much as; (after comparatives) than; with *tam* (see *tam*)

quamdiu (adv.)—as long as

quamquam (conj.)—though, although

quando (adv. and conj.)—when. Also for *aliquando*

quandocumque (adv.)—whenever, as often as

quandoque (adv.)—whenever

quandoquidem (adv.)—since, seeing that

quantopere (adv.)—how greatly

quantum (adv.)—as much as, so much as

quantus, -a, -um (adj.)—how great, how much; with *tantus* (see *tantus*)

quare (adv.)—wherefore

quarta, -e (f.)—quart; farthing

quarterius, -ii (m.)—quarter

quartus, -a, -um (adj.)—fourth

quasso (see *casso*)

quatenus (adv.)—how far, to what extent

quater (adv.)—four times

quatinus (adv. with verbs of asking and commanding)—that

quattuor—four

quattuordecim—fourteen

quasi (adv.)—as if, just as

-que (added to end of word)—and

quemadmodum (adv.)—in what manner, how, just as

quercus, -us (f.)—an oak

querela, -e (f.)—plaint, suit, action; fine paid by tenants

querelo (1)—to bring an action, implead, complain

querens, -entis (m., f., gen.pl. -ium)—plaintiff

quero, -ere, quesivi, quesitum (3)—to seek, ask

queror, queri, questus sum (3, depon.)—to complain

questus, -us (m.)—acquisition, property acquired

qui, que, quod (pron.)—who, which, what

quia (conj.)—because; whereas

quicquid (see *quisquis*)

quicumque, quecumque, quodcumque (pron.)—whosoever, whatsoever

quidam, quedam, quoddam (pron.)—a certain person or thing

quidem (adv.)—indeed, but, however; in truth

quietaclamantia, -ie (f.)—quitclaim. Also *quietaclamatio, -ionis* (f.)

quiete (adv.)—quietly, peacefully

quietius (adv.)—more quietly

quietumclamo (1)—to quitclaim

quietus, -a, -um (adj.)—quit, free

quietus, -us (m.)—receipt

quilibet, quelibet, quodlibet (pron.)—anyone you like, anyone at all, each; (plural) everyone whatsoever

quindecim—fifteen

quindena, -e (f.)—period of 15 days; the 15th day inclusive

quingenti, -e, -a (pl.)—five hundred

quinque—five

quintus, -a, -um (adj.)—fifth

quippe (adv. and conj.)—surely, indeed, inasmuch as

quis, quis, quid—who? which? what? (Kennedy, p. 32)

quis, quis, quid (pron. after *si, ne, nisi, cum*)—anyone, anything, someone, something

quisque (Kennedy, p. 33)—each one

quisquis, quisquis, quicquid (pron.)—whosoever, whatsoever quittantia, -ie (f.)—quittance, immunity

quitto (1)—to quit, to discharge

quittus, -a, -um (adj.)—quit, free

quivis, quevis, quodvis (or quidvis) (pron.)—anyone you like, anyone anything,

quo (adv.)—wherefore; whither; so that

quoad (adv.)—as long as, as far as

quocirca (conj.)—wherefore

quocumque (adv.)—whithersoever

quod (conj.)—because; (after verbs of knowing, saying, etc.) that

quomodo (adv.)—in what manner

quondam (adv.)—formerly; the late, the former. Also condam

quoniam (adv.)—whereas, since

quoque (conj.)—also

quotiens (adv.)—as often as; with totiens (see totiens)

quotienscumque (adv.)—as often soever as

quousque (adv.)—how long, how far; as long as, as far as, until

quovismodo (adv.)—in any way whatsoever

rata, -e (f.)—share, proportion; agreement

rate (adv.)—duly

ratifico (1)—to ratify

ratio, -ionis (f.)—reason; cause; account

ratiocinatio, -ionis (f.)—reckoning, account

rationabilis, -e (adv.)—reasonable, rational; regular, in due form

rationabiliter (adv.)—regularly, in due form

rato (1)—to assess; to ratify

ratus, -a, -um (adj.)—right, valid

realis, -e (adj.)—real (as in 'real estate')

realiter (adv.)—really, actually, with regard to real property

reassumo, -ere, -sumpsi, -sumptum (3)—to reassume

recedo, -ere, -cessi, -cessum (3)—to withdraw; to desist

recepta, -e (f.)—receipt, money received. Also receptum, -i (n.)

receptor, -oris (m.)—receiver (of money)

recetto (1)—to receive; to reset (leg.). Also recepto

recipio, -ere, -cepi, -ceptum (3)—to get back, recover, receive, accept

reclamo (1)—to claim; to declare; to confess; to oppose purgation

recognitio, -ionis (f.)—examination, inquest by jury; judgement of court or explanatory statement; acknowledgement of debt or obligation

recognosco, -ere, -gnovi, -gnitum (3)—to recognize, to acknowledge, to certify, to examine, to investigate by jury

recompenso (1)—to reward, recompense, compensate for, make good

reconventio, -ionis (f.)—resummons, counter-petition (leg.)

recordum, -i (n.)—record

recte (adv.)—rightly

rectitudo, -dinis (f.)—right, due, service. Also rectum, -i (n.)

rector, -oris (m.)—rector (eccles.)

rectum, -i (n.)—right, justice; see also rectitudo

rectus, -a, -um (adj.)—right; direct (of heirs)

recupero (1)—to recover
r. super, or r. versus—to recover from

recursus, -us (m.)—recourse

recuso (1)—to decline, reject, refuse, be unwilling to do

recussus (for rescussus)

redditio, -ionis (f.)—giving up, surrender, rendering

redditualis, -e (adj.)—of or for rent

redditus, -us (m.)—rent, revenue

   r. *assissus*—rent of assize or fixed rent

redditus, -a, -um (past part. of *reddo*)

reddo, -ere, -didi, -ditum (3)—to give back, to pay, surrender, hand over; to return, yield (profits, rent, etc.)

redelibero (1)—to deliver back, return

redemptio, -ionis (f.)—fine or relief

redigo, -ere, -egi, -actum (3)—to drive back; to reduce

refero, -ferre, -tuli, -latum (3)—to bring back, tell, relate, report; (with *ad*) to refer to

regalis, -e (adj.)—royal

regalitas, -atis (f.)—royal power, dignity, right

regina, -e (f.)—queen

registrum, -i (n.)—register; registry

regius, -a, -um (adj.)—royal

regnum, -i (n.)—kingdom, reign

regratator, -oris (m.)—a regrater

reingredior, -gredi, -gressus sum (3, depon.)—to re-enter

reintro (1)—to re-enter

relaxatio, -ionis (f.)—release, remittance, discharge

relaxo (1)—to release, remit, discharge; to commute

relevamentum, -i (n.)—relief, feudal due. Also *relevium, -ii* (n.)

relevio (1)—to pay a relief for. Also *relevo* (1)

relicta, -e (f.)—widow

relictus, -a, -um (adj.)—remaining

relinquo, -ere, -liqui, -lictum (3)—to leave, relinquish, bequeath

reliquus, -a, -um (adj.)—remaining

remanentia, -e (f.)—remainder

remaneo, -ere, remansi (2)—to remain behind; to pass to another owner on the death of the first, or on other specified conditions

remanerium, -ii (n.)—remainder (leg.)

remissio, -ionis (f.)—remission, written grant

remitto, -ere, -misi, -missum (3)—to remise

renovatio, -ionis (f.)—renewal

   r. *arcis*—burgbote

renovo (1)—to renew, restore

rentale, -is (n.)—rental; rent-book

reparatio, -ionis (f.)—repairing, repairs

reparo (1)—to repair

repello, -ere, reppuli, repulsum (3)—to drive back, repel

reperio, -ire, repperi, repertum (4)—to find

reprisa (f.)—deduction

reputatus, -a, -um (past part.)—considered, reputed, deemed

reputo (1)—to consider, reckon

requies, -etis (f.)—rest

requiesco, -ere, -evi, -etum (3)—to rest

res, rei (f.)—thing, matter, business

   res divina—divine service

rescussus, -us (m.)—illegal recovery of goods or persons from custody, 'rescue'

rescutio, -ere, -cussi, -cussum (3)—to 'rescue' (see *rescussus*)

reservatio, -ionis (f.)—reservation of benefices; reservation of a case in eccles. court

residuus, -a, -um (adj.)—remaining

   residuum, -ui (n.)—the residue

resigno (1)—to resign, surrender

respecto (1)—to adjourn, postpone. Also *respectuo* (1)

respectus, -us (m.)—adjournment, postponement, respite. Also *respectum, -i* (n.)

respondeo, -ere, -spondi, -sponsum (2)—to reply, answer; (with *de* or *pro*) to be answerable for

responsalis, -e (adj.)—answerable for or to; of or for a reply *responsalis, -is* (m.)—deputy, representative

responsum, -i (n.)—answer, reply

restitutus, -a, -um (past part.)—replaced, restored

retenementum, -i (n.)—reservation. Also *retinementum*

retineo, -ere, -tinui, retentum (2)—to retain, preserve

retraho, -ere, -traxi, -tractum (3)—to draw back; (with *se*) to withdraw (oneself) from suit (leg.)

retro (adv. and pre. with acc.)—backwards, behind, formerly; in arrears

a retro esse—to be in arrears

reventiones, -um (f.pl.)—revenue. Also *reventus, -us* (m.)

reverencia, -e (f.)—reverence

reversatio, -ionis (f.)—reversion of property, right of reversion. Also *reversio, -ionis* (f.)

reverto, -ere, -verti, -versum (3)—to turn back, to revert. Also *revertor, -ti, reversus sum* (3, depon.)

rex, regis (m.)—king

ribaldus, -a, -um (adj.)—ribald, lewd

ribaldus, -i (m.)—low fellow, rascal

ripa, -e (f.)—bank (of river)

riparia, -e (f.)—river or river bank

robor, -oris (n.)—force, power. Also *robur, -oris* (n.)

roboro (1)—to strengthen, to confirm

roda, -e (f.)—rood (measure of land)

Rogerus, -i (m.)—Roger

ropa, -e (f.)—'rope', measurement (20 ft.)

rosa, -e (f.)—rose

rota, -e (f.)—a wheel

rotulatio, -ionis (f.)—enrolment, entry on roll

rotulus, -i (m.)—roll, record. Also *rotullus*

ruber, -bra, -brum (adj.)—red. Also *rubius, -a, -um*

rumpo, -ere, rupi, ruptum (3)—to break, burst

Sabbati dies, dies Sabbatina—Saturday

saca, -e (f.)—sac, form of jurisdiction

sacerdos, -dotis (m.)—priest

sacerdotalis, -e (adj.)—priestly

sacramentalia, -ium (n.pl.)—sacramentals

sacramentarium, -ii (n.)—sacrament

sacramentum, -i (n.)—corporal oath; sacrament

sacrista, -e (m.)—sacristan

sacristia, -ie (f.)—sacristy

sacrosancta, -orum (n.pl.)—holy objects (as Gospel-book) used for touching in oath-taking

sacrum, -i (n.)—corporal oath

saisina (see *seisina*)

saisio (see *seiso*)

sal, salis (m.)—salt

salarium, -ii (n.)—stipend of an eccles. benefice

salubris, -e (adj.)—wholesome; beneficial

salus, -utis (f.)—safety, salvation; salutation, greeting

salvo (1)—to save

salvus, -a, -um (adj.)—safe; especially in abl. absolute—saving, without violation of, excepting only

sancta, -orum (n.pl.)—holy objects to be touched in oath-taking

sanctimonialis, -is (adj. used as noun)—religious person, nun, monk

sanctitas, -tatis (f.)—holiness

sanctus, -a, -um (adj.)—holy; saint

sanguis, sanguinis (m.)—blood

sanus, -a, -um (adj.)—healthy

sarclatio, -ionis (f.)—weeding

sarclio (1)—to hoe, to weed, to sow. Also *sarclo; sarculo*

sarto (1)—to assart

sartum, -i (n.)—an assart or forest-clearing

satis (adv.)—sufficiently, enough; very

satisfacio, -ere, -feci, -factum (3)—to satisfy, give satisfaction

scaccarium, -ii (n.)—exchequer

schedula (see *cedula*)

schopa (see *shopa*)

sciencia, -e (f.)—knowledge

scilicet (adv.)—clearly, certainly, namely, to wit

scio, scire, scivi, scitum (4)—to know

scira (see *shira*)

scituans (see *situans*)

scituatus (see *situatus*)

scitus, -us (m.)—site

scotum, -i (n.)—scot, payment

scriptorium, -ii (n.)—scriptorium; registry

scriptum, -i (n.)—writing, deed, bond

scrutator, -oris (m.)—examiner, investigator, 'searcher'

scrutinentia, -e (f.)—scrutiny, esp. of documents or exhibits in a case

scrutor (1, depon.)—to examine, investigate

scuratio, -ionis (f.)—scouring

scuro (see *escuro*)

scutagium, -ii (n.)—scutage

scyra (see *shira*)

se (reflexive pron.)—himself, herself, itself, themselves

seco, -are, secui, sectum (1)—to cut

secretarius, -ii (m.)—secretary, clerk

secta, -e (f.)—suit of court; body of witnesses produced in court (leg.)

secularis, -e (adj.)—secular

seculum, -i (n.)—lifetime, an age, this world, this life

  in seculum, in secula; in seculum seculi; in secula seculorum—to all eternity, forever

secundum (adv. and prep. with acc.)—after, afterwards, according to

secundus, -a, -um (adj.)—second, following

securitas, -tatis (f.)—safety, security; making safe, preserving

sed or *set* (conj.)—but

sedecim—sixteen

sedecimus, -a, -um (adj.)—sixteenth

sedeo, -ere, sedi, sessum (2)—to sit; to hold eccles. office or property; to be convenient or suitable

sedes, -is (f., gen.pl. *-ium*)—seat, see, site

sedile, -is (n.)—chair, bench, pew

sedua (see *silva*)

seisina, -e (f.)—seisin. Also *saisina*

seiso (1)—to seize, put in possession

  saisio (1)—to seize, take possession of

selda, -e (f.)—stall, shop

selio, -ionis (f.)—ridge, strip, measure of ploughland. Also *seillo, seillum*

sella, -e (f.)—seat, chair, stool

semel (adv.)—once

semino (1)—to sow

semita, -e (f.)—lane, footpath

sempiternus, -a, -um (adj.)—everlasting

senecallus, -i (m.)—seneschal, steward

senior, -ioris (adj. and noun; gen.pl. *-um*)—older; elder; the elder

sententia, -e (f.)—sentence of a law-court

separabile, -is (n., decl. Kennedy, p. 16, §31)—severalty. Also *separale, -is* (n.); *separalitas, -itatis* (f.)

separalis, -e (adj.)—several, separate, individual

separaliter (adv.)—severally, separately

sepe (adv.)—often

sepedictus, -a, -um (adj.)—oft-mentioned

sepes, -is (f., gen.pl. *-ium*)—hedge, fence

sepio, -ire, -psi, -ptum (4)—to enclose, hedge in

septem—seven

septendecim—seventeen

septentrio, -ionis (m.)—the north. Also septentriones, -onum (plural form often used)

septentrionalis, -e (adj.)—northern

septimana, -e (f.)—a week

Septimana penosa—Holy Week

septimus, -a, -um (adj.)—seventh

septingenti, -e, -a—seven hundred

septuaginta—seventy

sepultura, -e (f.)—burial; right of burial, fee for burial

sepultus, -a, -um (past part.)—buried

sequela, -e (f.)—family or household of a serf; suit of court; right to pursue

sequens, -entis (pres. part)—following

sequens, -entis (m., f., gen.pl. -ium)—suitor to a court

sequentia, -e (f.)—suit

sequestrator, -oris (m.)—sequestrator

sequestrum -i (n.)—sequestration

sequor, sequi, secutus sum (3, depon.)—to follow; to pay suit of court. Also s. curiam; s. placitum

serenus, -a, -um (adj.)—serene

serenissimus, -a, -um (adj.)—most serene

seriatim (adv.)—in order, in succession

sericum, -i (n.)—silk

seriose (adv.)—in detail

serjantia, -ie (f.)—serjeanty; land held by serjeanty

Serlo, -onis (m.)—Serlo (proper name)

servicium, -ii (n.)—villein tenure; service

serviens, -ientis (m., f., gen.pl. -ium)—servant; tenant under the rank of knight holding land by military service; serjeant. Also as present part., with object in dative—serving

servilis, -e (adj.)—involving the services or status of a villein

servisia (see cervisia)

servo (1)—to preserve, keep, protect, guard

servus, -i (m.)—serf, villein

sescenti, -e, -a—six hundred

set (see sed)

seu (see sive)

sex—six

sexaginta—sixty

sextarium, -ii (n.)—sester, dry or liquid measure

sextus, -a, -um (adj.)—sixth

shira, -e (f.)—shire. Also scira; scyra; sira

shopa, -e (f.)—shop, workshop

si (conj.)—if; whether

sic (adv.)—thus, so; 'yes'

sicut (adv.)—just as

sigillatio, -ionis (f.)—sealing

sigillo (1)—to seal

sigillum,-i (n.)—seal; sealed document

signatio, -ionis (f.)—marking, stamping, sealing

signatura, -e (f.)—sign, mark, stamp, sign-manual

significatum, -i (n.)—meaning

signo (1)—to mark, to stamp

signum, -i (n.)—sign, device (on documents); bell

sikettus, -i (m.)—dyke, syke

siligo, -inis (f.)—rye

silva, -e (f.)—a wood

s. cedua, s. sedua—coppice-wood

similis, -e (adj.)—like, similar

similiter (adv.)—similarly

Simo or Simon, Simonis (m.)—Simon

simul (adv.)—at the same time, together, also, likewise

sin (conj.)—if however, if on the contrary, but if

sine (prep. with abl.)—without

singuli, -e, -a (pl., adj.)—each separate one, every single one

sinister, -tra, -trum (adj.)—left

sinistre (adv.)—on the left side

sira (see shira)

situatio, -ionis (f.)—site. Also situatum, -i (n.)

situatus, -a, -um (adj.)—situated

situs (see scitus)

sive (conj.)—or if, whether, or. Also seu

sive . . . sive (seu . . . seu)—whether . . . or; if . . . or if

soca, -e (f.)—soc. Also socum, -i (n.), socha, -e (f.)

socagium, -ii (n.)—soke; soccage

socmannus, -i (m.)—sokeman, tenant in soccage. Also sokemannus, -i (m.)

solarium, -ii (n.)—upper room; dwelling. Also solerium

solemniter (adv.)—solemnly

solempnizo (1)—to solemnize
s. matrimonium—to solemnize a marriage

soleo, -ere, solitus sum (2, semi-depon.) —to be accustomed

solidata, -e (f.)—a shilling's worth

solidum, -i (n.)—the whole sum
ex solido, in solido—wholly, completely

solidus, -i (m.)—a shilling

solum, -i (n.)—soil, earth, ground, land, floor

solummodo (adv.)—only

solutio, -ionis (f.)—payment

solvo, -ere, solvi, solutum (3)—to pay; to relax a sentence; to end a visitation (eccles.)

soror, -oris (f.)—sister; nun

sororius, -ii (m.)—sister's husband or son

sors, sortis (f., gen.pl. -ium)—a lot, casting of lots; share

specialis, -e (adj.)—special; private, confidential

specialiter (adv.)—specifically

specifico (1)—to specify

specto (1)—to look to, to face, to be situated towards some quarter; to belong to, to pertain or have regard to

spiritualis, -e (adj.)—spiritual, ecclesiastical

sponsa, -e (f.)—wife

sponsalia (n.pl., gen. -ium)—marriage dues, marriage banns

sponsalicia (n.pl., gen. -ium)—marriage

sponso (1)—to marry

sponsus, -i (m.)—husband

sponte (adv.)—freely, voluntarily

stabilis, -e (adj.)—valid

stagnum, -i (n.)—pond

stapula, -e (f.)—staple

stallum, -i (n.)—market-stall

statim (adv.)—immediately, at once

status, -us (m.)—state; estate; legal rights in property; inventory

statutio, -ionis (f.)—statute
s. mercatorum, s. stapule—statute-merchant, statute-staple

staurum, -i (n.)—stock

sterlingus, -a, -um (adj.)—sterling

sterlingus, -i (m.)—silver penny
sterlingi, -orum (m.pl.)—sterlings

sterquilinium, -ii (n.)—dung-heap, dung-pit

stipendium, -ii (n.)—stipend, hiring, wages

stipes, -itis (m.)—log, post; offertory-box

stipula, -e (f.)—stalk, straw, stubble

sto, stare, steti, statum (1)—to stand; to be, remain, occur; to stand, to be valid

strata, -e (f.)—way, road
s. alta—highway
s. regia—king's highway

strekum, -i (n.)—a strike, dry measure. Also estreca, esterium

strictura, -e (f.)—distraint

studeo, -ere, -ui (2)—to study; to apply oneself to

studium, -ii (n.)—study; room for study; zeal
studium generale—university

sub (prep. with acc. and abl.)—under, below; towards; shortly before, just after; during

 sub pena—on pain of

 sub manibus—in hand

 sub virga—under the control of

subballivus, -i (m.)—under-bailiff

subboscus, -i (m.)—underwood, coppice-wood

subditus, -i (m.)—member of a priest's flock; subject of an eccles. official

sub-forestarius, -ii (m.)—under-forester

submersus, -a, -um (past part.)—under water, flooded, drowned

submitto, -ere, -misi, -missum (3)—to lower; to subjugate; to propose; to claim, to offer to prove

subscribo, -ere, -psi, -ptum (3)—to write underneath, subscribe a document

subsequenter (adv.)—subsequently, afterwards

subsidium, -ii (n.)—payment, subsidy, feudal aid

substitutus, -i (m.)—substitute; bishop's ordinary; proctor

subter (adv. and prep. with acc. and abl.)—below, underneath

subtus (adv. and prep. with acc. and abl.)—below, underneath, behind

successio, -ionis (f.)—descendants (collective noun)

successive (adv.)—successively, in succession

successivus, -a, -um (adj.)—successive, following

successor, -oris (m.)—successor, descendant

succido, -ere, -cidi, -cisum (3)—to fell, cut down

sufficiens, -tis (adj.)—sufficient, adequate

sufficientia, -e (f.)—a sufficiency

suggestum, -i (n.)—pulpit

sum, esse, fui (*essendum*, gerund)—to be

summa, -e (f.)—sum

summarius, -ii (m.)—sumpter horse

summoneo, -ere, -monui, -monitum (2)—to summon

summonitio, -ionis (f.)—summons

sumptus, -us (m.) or *sumptus, -i* (m.)—expense, cost, charge

super (indecl. adj.)—above-mentioned

super (adv. and prep. with acc. and abl.)—above, upon; on, at, against, in (of time and place); on pain of; in accordance with

superinde (adv.)—on that account; in respect thereof

superior, -ioris (m.)—superior, feudal overlord

superior, superius (adj.; Kennedy, pp. 24, §49)—higher, upper, previous

superius (adv.)—previously, above

supernominatus, -a, -um (adj.)—above-named

superstes, -stitis (adj.; decl. Kennedy p. 23)—surviving

supervisor, -oris (m.)—inspector, overseer; surveyor

supplico (1)—to beseech

suppono, -ere, -posui, -positum (3)—to suppose, assume

supra (adv. and prep. with acc.)—above, beyond, before

supradico, -ere, -dixi, -dictum (3)—to mention above

supradictus, -a, -um (adj., past part.)—above-mentioned

suprascriptus, -a, -um (past part.)—above-written

sursum (adv.)—up, upwards

sursumredditio, -ionis (f.)—surrender, giving up

sursumreddo, -ere, -reddidi, -redditum (3)—to surrender, give up

sus, suis (m., f.)—pig, sow

suscipio, -ere, -cepi, -ceptum (3)—to receive, accept, take possession of

suspendo- -ere -di, -sum (3)—to hang, suspend; to suspend from sacraments (eccles.)

sustentatio, -ionis (f.)—support, maintenance

sustentator, -oris (m.)—one who supports or maintains

sustineo, -ere, -tinui (or *sustinevi*), *-tentum* (2)—to support, maintain

sutor, -oris (m.)—cobbler

suus, sua, suum (adj.)—one's own; his, her, its, their

synodus, -i (f.)—synod (eccles. assembly)

taberna, -e (f.)—tavern, inn

talea, -e (f.)—tally, tax, entail

talis, -e (adj.)—such

    talis . . . qualis—such . . . as

tallagium, -ii (n.)—tallage

tallia, -e (f.)—tally

talliata, -e (f.)—tax, tallage

tallo (1)—to entail

tam (adv.)—so, so much, as

    tam . . . quam—so . . . as, as . . . as, both . . . and

tamdiu (adv.)—so long, for so long a time

tamen (adv.)—nevertheless, however; yet; though

tametsi (conj.)—notwithstanding that, although, and yet

tamquam (adv.)—as much as, so as, as it were, so to speak, as if, as

tandem (adv.)—at length, finally

tango, tangere, tetigi, tactum (3)—to touch; to concern

tantum (adv.)—so much, so greatly, so; only, merely

    tantum . . . quantum—as . . . as, so much . . . as

tantumdem (adv.)—just so much

tantummodo (adv.)—only so much

tantus, -a, -um (adj.)—so great

tantus . . . quantus—so great . . . as, as great . . . as

tasso (1)—to stack

tastator, -oris (m.)—ale-taster

taxo (1)—to tax; assess for taxation; to assess fees or expenses

tedinga (see *tethinga*)

temporale, -is (n., decl. Kennedy, p. 16, §31)—temporal right or business. Also *temporalitas, -tatis* (f.)

temporalis, -e (adj.)—temporal, lay

temporaliter (adv.)—with regard to temporal things

tempus, temporis (n.)—time, period

tenatura, -e (f.)—feudal holding, tenement, tenure

tenementum, -i (n.)—feudal holding, tenement, tenure, house

tenens, -entis (m., f., gen.pl. *-ium*)—tenant; defendant

teneo, -ere, tenui, tentum (2)—to hold, hold land, to bind, oblige

    t. debitum—to owe

tenor, -oris (m.)—an uninterrupted course, career, tenor; the contents, sense or tenor of an agreement, law or document

tentio, -ionis (f.)—holding a court

tentus, -a, -um (past part.)—held

tenura, -e (f.)—feudal holding, tenure

tenus (prep. with abl.)—as far as

ter (adv.)—three times

terminarius, -ii (m.)—lessee

termino (1)—to terminate; to determine, to define, to decide cases (leg.)

terminus, -i (m.)—limit, boundary, end, term, period, time-limit

terra, -e (f.)—land, piece of land' tenement, strip

    terra sacra—cemetery, churchyard

terrarium, -ii (n.)—terrier

terrarius, -a, -um (adj.)—land-owning

terrenus, -a, -um (adj.)—pertaining to land; land-owning

terrenus, -i (m.)—tenant

territorium, -i (n.)—district, territory

tertius, -a, -um (adj.)—third

testamentum, -i (n.)—will, testament

testifico (1)—to bear witness to

testimonium, -ii (n.)—testimony; compurgation

testis (m., f., gen.pl. *-ium*)—a witness

testor (1, depon.)—to witness

tethinga, -e (f.)—tithing. Also *tedinga, -e* (f.)

textus, -us (m.)—text, document, charter

thalamus, -i (m.)—chamber, bed-chamber

thanagium, -ii (n.)—thanage

thainus, -i (m.)—thane. Also *thanus, -i* (m.)

Thomas, -am, -e, -e, -a (m.)—Thomas

tignum, -i (n.)—a beam, timber

tipulator, -oris (m.)—a tippler

titulus, -i (m.)—title, claim

tofta, -e (f.)—toft; house-place. Also *toftum, -i* (n.)

tonsio, -ionis (f.)—sheep-shearing, cutting

torale, -is (n., Kennedy, p. 16, §31)—kiln

torus, -i (m.)—couch, bed; wedlock

tot . . . quot—so many . . . as

totalis, -e (adj.)—entire

totaliter (adv.)—entirely

totiens . . . quotiens—as often . . . as

totus, -a, -um (adj.)—the whole, all, the entire

traditio, -ionis (f.)—handing over, surrender, demise; formal written conveyance

trado, -ere, tradidi, traditum (3)—to hand over, leave, demise

    t. ad firmam—to farm, to let at farm

traho, -ere, traxi, tractum (3)—to draw, haul

    t. moram—to tarry; to live

tramesium, tramagium, tramasium (see *tremesium*)

transgressio, -ionis (f.)—offence, trespass, transgression. Also *transgressus, -us* (m.)

transitus, -us (m.)—a passing over, passing away; death

translatio, -ionis (f.)—transferring, translation

transmitto, -ere, -misi, -missum (3)—to despatch, transmit; to hand over

trebuchettum, -i (n.)—ducking-stool

trecenti, -e, -a—three hundred

tredecim—thirteen

tremesium, -ii (n.)—summer corn, summer sowing

trenchea, -e (f.)—trench, ditch, moat; forest clearing. Also *trencata, -e* (f.)

tres, trium—three

tresdecim—thirteen

triatio, -ionis (f.)—trial

tricesimus, -a, -um (adj.)—thirtieth

triennium, -ii (n.)—a three-year period; three years

triginta—thirty

Trinitas, -itatis (f.)—Trinity

    T. Sancta—Holy Trinity; Trinity Sunday

trio (1)—to try (leg.)

tripartitus, -a, -um (adj.)—threefold, tripartite

trituro (1)—to thresh

truncus, -i (m.)—'trunk' for free-will offerings

tuicio, -ionis (f.)—protection; defence

tum (adv.)—then

tumulatus, -a, -um (past part.)—buried

tunc (adv.)—then

    tunc temporis—at that time

tunica, -e (f.)—tunicle (eccles.)

turba, -e (f.)—turf

turbarium, *-ii* (n.)—turbary, turf-pit. Also *turbaria*, *-e* (f.)

tute (adv.)—safely, securely

tutius (adv.)—more securely

tutela, *-e* (f.)—guardianship, wardship

tuto (adv.)—safely, securely

tutus, *-a*, *-um* (adj.)—safe, secure

tuus, *-a*, *-um* (adj.)—thine, yours

uber, *-eris* (adj.)—fertile, abundant

ubi (adv.)—where; when

ubicumque (adv.)—wheresoever

ubique (adv. and also as adj.)—everywhere, wheresoever

ullus, *-a*, *-um* (pron. and adj.)—any, anyone

ulna, *-e* (f.)—elbow; an ell

ulterior, *ulterius* (adj., Kennedy, p. 24, §49)—farther, on the farther side, beyond

ulterius (adv.)—for the future; furthermore

ultimo (adv.)—lately, recently

ultimus, *-a*, *-um* (adj.)—the farthest, the last, the latest

ultra (adv. and prep. with acc.)—on the other side, beyond, farther; over and above (of amounts)

umquam (see *unquam*)

una cum—together with

unanimis, *-e* (adj.)—of one mind, unanimous

uncea, *-e* (f.); *uncia*, *-e* (f.)—ounce; inch

unde (adv.)—whence, wherefore, wherewith, whereof, whereupon; concerning which, in respect whereof

undecim—eleven

undecimus, *-a*, *-um* (adj.)—eleventh

undetricesimus, *-a*, *-um* (adj.)—twenty-ninth

undetriginta—twenty-nine

undevicesimus, *-a*, *-um* (adj.)—nineteenth

undeviginti—nineteen

undique (adv.)—from all parts, on all sides, everywhere

unicus, *-a*, *-um* (adj.)—only, sole

universalis, *-e* (adj.)—universal

universaliter (adv.)—universally, without exception

universitas, *-itatis* (f.)—the whole
u. vestra—all ye

universus, *-a*, *-um* (adj.)—the whole, all

unquam (adv.)—ever. Also *umquam*

unus, *-a*, *-um* (pron. and adj.)—one; a, an

urcea, *-e* (f.)—cruet (eccles.)

usagium, *-ii* (n.)—use, usage, right to use

usitatio, *-ionis* (f.)—use, usage

usitatus, *-a*, *-um* (past part.)—wonted, customary, accustomed

usito (1)—to use

usque (adv.)—as far as, until, up to

usualis, *-e* (adj.)—usual

usualiter (adv.)—usually

usufructus, *-us* (m.)—usufruct, use and enjoyment of property belonging to another

usus, *-us* (m.)—use; right of possession

ut (adv. and conj.)—as; that, in order that

utensilia, *-ium* (n.pl.)—appurtenances, easements; necessaries

uterque, *utraque*, *utrumque* (pron.)—each (of two), either, both

utilitas, *-tatis* (f.)—advantage, benefit

utor, *uti*, *usus sum* (3, depon. with object in abl.)—to use

utpote (adv.)—namely, inasmuch as

utputa (adv.)—as for instance, namely, as for example

utrimque (adv.)—on both sides, from both sides. Also *utrumque*

utrum (adv.)—whether

utrumque (see *utrimque*)

uxor, *-oris* (f.)—wife

uxoratus, -i (m.)—married man

uxoratus, -a (past part.)—married

uxoro (1) and *uxoror* (1, depon.)—to marry; to give in marriage

vacatio, -ionis (f.)—exemption, immunity; vacancy; annulling

vacca, -e (f.)—cow

vaccaria, -e (f.)—cowpasture; cowshed

vaco (1)—to be vacant; to be void, of no effect

vacuo (1)—to annul

vacuus, -a, -um (adj.)—vacant, empty

vadio (1)—to give security for; to give as security

   v. misericordiam—to put oneself at mercy

vadium, -ii (n.)—pledge, security

vado, -ere, vadi (3)—to go

vagabundus, -i (m.)—vagabond

valde (adv.)—exceedingly

valens, -entis (n.)—value. Also *valentia, -e* (f.)

valeo, -ere, valui, -itum (2)—to be strong; to be capable of, able to; to be valid; to be worth; to flourish or prosper; to have power to

validus, -a, -um (adj.)—strong, effective, valid

valor, -oris (m.)—value

vannatarius, -ii (m.)—a winnower. Also *vannator, -oris* (m.)

vario (1)—to divert or alienate property

vassallus, -i (m.)—vassal

vastatio, -ionis (f.)—waste, damage. Also *vastum, -i* (n.)

veho, -ere, vexi, vectum (3)—to carry

vel (conj.)—or, or else. Also *vell*

   vel . . . vel—either . . . or

velle (infinitive of *volo*)—to wish

velle (indeclin., n.)—will, testament. Also *velleum, -i* (n.)

velut (adv.)—just as; for example

venacio, -ionis (f.)—hunting, hunting-rights

vendicatio, -ionis (f.)—claiming

vendico (1)—to lay legal claim to; to liberate, to protect; to avenge. Also *vindico*

venditio, -ionis (f.)—sale, right of sale; felled wood

venditus, -a, -um (past part.)—sold; compounded for; allowed to compound for fine; commuted

vendo, -ere, vendidi, venditum (3)—to sell

venella, -e (f.)—a lane

venerabilis, -e (adj.)—venerable

veneris (see *die*)

venio, -ire, veni, ventum (4)—to come

verbero (1)—to beat

verbum, -i (n.)—word

vere (adv.)—truly

veredictum, -i (n.)—verdict; presentment under oath

veritas, -tatis (f.)—truth

verius (adv.)—more truly

vero (adv.)—truly, in fact; however

versus (adv.)—towards, facing

verto, -ere, -ti, -sum (3)—to turn

verus, -a, -um (adj.)—true

vester, -tra, -trum (adj.)—your

vestis, -is (f.)—vestment; set of vestments

vestitus, -a, -um (adj.)—bearing a crop

vestura, -e (f.)—a crop

vetus, -eris (adj., decl. Kennedy, p. 23)—old

via, -e (f.)—way, road

   v. alta—highway

   v. publica—public highway

   v. regia—king's highway

viaticus, -i (m.)—wayfarer, tramp

vicaria, -e (f.)—office or benefice of a vicar. Also *vicariatus, -us* (m.)

vicarius, -ii (m.)—vicar

vice (see *vicis*)

vicecomes -itis (m.)—sheriff, reeve

vicecomitatus, -us (m.)—district administered by a sheriff, shrievalty

vicem (see *vicis*)

vicesimus, -a, -um (adj.)—twentieth

viciatus, -i (m.)—bastard

vicinagium, -ii (n.)—vicinage

vicinetum, -i (n.)—neighbourhood; venue; jury of the venue

vicinus, -a, -um (adj.)—neighbouring

vicinus, -i (m.)—neighbour; farmer

vicinum, -i (n.)—neighbourhood, vicinity

viciosus, -a, -um (adj.)—faulty, defective

vicis (f., decl. Kennedy, p. 20)—time, occasion, change, alteration

   invicem (adv.)—by turns, alternately, reciprocally, respectively

   vice—instead, for, on account of

   per vices—from time to time, at various times

vicus, -i (m.)—street; city quarter

videlicet (adv.)—clearly, evidently, to wit, namely; that is

video, -ere, vidi, visum (2)—to see, to view, to inspect

vidua, -e (f.)—widow

viduetas, -tatis (f.)—widowhood

   v. legitima, v. libera, v. ligia, v. pura—complete power of disposition possessed by a widow

viduus, -i (m.)—widower

vigeo, -ere, -ui (2)—to flourish; to be in esteem

vigilatio, -ionis (f.)—watching, eve of a festival. Also *vigilia, -e* (f.)

viginti—twenty

vigor, -oris (m.)—strength, validity, force

villa, -e (f.)—vill, town, township. Also *villata, -e* (f.)

villanus, -i (m.)—villein

villenagium, -ii (n.)—villenage; land held by villein tenure

vimen, -inis (n.)—osier, withy, basket

vinagium, -ii (n.)—custom on wine or vineyards

vinarium, -ii (n.)—vineyard

vinculum, -i (n.)—chain

vindico (see *vendico*)

vinea, -e (f.)—vineyard. Also *vinetum, -i* (n.)

vinum, -i (n.)—wine

vir, viri (m.)—man; husband

virga, -e (f.)—virgate, yardland; a yard; verge, jurisdiction of a court. Also *virgata, -e* (f.)

viridis, -e (adj.)—green

virtus, -tutis (f.)—strength, virtue, force or effect of a document

vis (f., decl. Kennedy, p. 15)—strength, power, meaning, force

visnetum, -i (n., for *vicinetum*)

visuri, -orum (m.pl.)—those about to see

visus, -us (m.)—look, view

vita, -e (f.)—life

vitiosus (see *viciosus*)

vito (1)—to avoid

vitula, -e (f.), *vitulus, -i* (m.)—calf

vitulina, -e (f.)—veal

vivarium, -ii (n.)—fish-pond, preserve, park

vivens, -tis (pres. part. and noun, m., f.)—living; liver

vivo, -ere, vixi, victum (3)—to live

vivus, -a, -um (adj.)—alive, living, live

vocatus, -a, -um (past part.)—called, named

voco (1)—to call, to name, to vouch, to call as evidence

volo, velle, volui—to wish, intend, be willing

voluntas, -atis (f.)—wish, will, testament; meaning, import of speech or writing

vos, vestrum (pron.)—you

vulneratura, -e (f.)—wounding

vulnero (1)—to wound

wainabilis, -e (adj.)—capable of yield-
  ing profits
wainagium, -ii (n.)—team of wagons
  or ploughs
wannagium, -ii (n.)—wainage, yield or
  profit of cultivated land
wapentachium, -ii (n.)—wapentake
warantia, -e (f.)—warranty. Also
  warantya
warantizatio, -ionis (f.)—warranty,
  guarantee
warantizo (1)—to warrant
warda, -e (f.)—guardianship of the
  person or estate of a minor; an
  estate in ward; service of watch
  and ward

wardus, -i (m.)—ward
warecta, -e (f.)—fallow land. Also
  waretus, -i (m.)
wastum, -i (n.)—waste; waste land
wavio (1)—to abandon, resign, waive
wera, -e (f.)—weir
wimplerius, -ii (m.)—wimple-maker
wlt (for *vult*)—he, she, it, wills, wishes
Wodenis (see *die*)

yconomus (for *oeconomus*)
ydoneus (for *idoneus*)
yems (for) *heims*

zona, -e (f.)—belt, girdle
zonarius, -ii (m.)—girdle-maker